CU00484910

SIZZLING I

'This book leaves you breathless! It's the personal story of energetic evangelism by a man who has been near to death but never crushed. It doesn't provide a blueprint for all Christians to copy, but it will make you ask what you are doing with the one life God has given you. . . I commend most warmly *Sizzling Faith*.'

The Most Reverend and Right Honourable Dr John Sentamu,
Archbishop of York

'I know this to be a true story of a truly amazing move of the Holy Spirit, with which I have been involved from almost the beginning. A breathtaking account of God's favour, his deliverance and an extraordinary harvest of multitudes around the world. A wonderful read—a real faith encourager.'

Robert Ward, Chairman of Youth for Christ North East,
and of Tyneside for Christ

'We have all read stirring missionary autobiographies, and most leave us open-mouthed and in awe. Martin Graham's account of his and Gina's remarkable achievements and sometimes almost non-existent faith, somehow seems to be more within the grasp of ordinary mortals like me. His story will, I'm sure, inspire many would-be evangelists to follow their dreams.'

John Noble, Pioneer Network and Chairman of Charismata,
The National Charismatic Leaders Conference

'It is a remarkable story, full of interventions from God, miracles of guidance, provision and indeed rescue in the context of cliff-edge situations. Repeatedly, all is risked towards the fulfilment of a very clear calling. The risks were worth taking because something of importance was being born. Now it has grown, literally worldwide. Read on, and be encouraged.'

Michael Green, author and pastor

'This is a very remarkable story. . . It is a fascinating testimony of what God will do with a truly dedicated and surrendered life. From businessman to evangelist, from Birmingham to the capital cities of all the major nations of the world, stepping out in faith with virtually no resources, and overcoming life-threatening illness, it is an unfolding lesson in the fruitfulness of hearing God and doing what he says. It is a powerful reminder in human testimony of God's great love of evangelism, and a spur to those who want to engage in it.'

Bob Dunnett
Pray for Revival

'A truly compelling story of God at work in the midst of vulnerability and hamburgers!'

Joel Edwards, General Director,
Evangelical Alliance

Sizzling Faith

MARTIN GRAHAM

KINGSWAY PUBLICATIONS
EASTBOURNE

Copyright © Martin Graham 2006

The right of Martin Graham to be identified as author of this work
has been asserted by him in accordance with the
Copyright, Designs and Patents Act 1988.

First published 2006

All rights reserved.
No part of this publication may be reproduced or
transmitted in any form or by any means, electronic
or mechanical, including photocopy, recording, or any
information storage and retrieval system, without
permission in writing from the publisher.

The publishers will permit up to 400 words of prose
to be extracted for non-commercial purposes or for review,
subject to full acknowledgement being given to author,
title of work, publisher's name and date of publication.

Unless otherwise stated, Scripture quotations are taken
from the New International Version ©; 1973, 1978, 1984
by the International Bible Society.
Verses marked RSV are from the Revised Standard Version
©; 1946, 1952, 1971, 1973 by the Division of
Christian Education and Ministry of the
National Council of the Churches of Christ in the USA.

Design for cover by CCD (www.ccdgroup.co.uk)

ISBN 1 84291 283 6
ISBN-13: 978–1–842912–83–6

01 02 03 04 05 06 Printing/Year 09 08 07 06

KINGSWAY COMMUNICATIONS LTD
Lottbridge Drove, Eastbourne BN23 6NT, England
Email: books@kingsway.co.uk
Printed in the USA

Dedication

For all those who came with us

Psalm 111

Praise the LORD.
I will extol the LORD with all my heart
in the council of the upright and in the assembly.
Great are the works of the LORD;
they are pondered by all who delight in them.
Glorious and majestic are his deeds,
and his righteousness endures for ever.
He has caused his wonders to be remembered;
the LORD is gracious and compassionate.
He provides food for those who fear him;
he remembers his covenant for ever.
He has shown his people the power of his works,
giving them the lands of other nations.
The works of his hands are faithful and just;
    all his precepts are trustworthy.
They are steadfast for ever and ever,
done in faithfulness and uprightness.
He provided redemption for his people;
    he ordained his covenant for ever –
    holy and awesome is his name.
The fear of the LORD is the beginning of wisdom;
all who follow his precepts have good understanding.
To him belongs eternal praise.

Contents

Part 4

Foreword

We were working together on a week of Christian outreach meetings in the north of England. Martin Graham was on the team—his first for this sort of thing. At that time he was Chief Executive of the Kent Chamber of Commerce and Industry.

As we reflected on the outreach in which we were engaged, he said something like this:

> 'I would love to see some modern form of attractive Christian witness in the open air. The old ways of street corner preaching no longer have any appeal. Indeed, they put people off. I am sure there is an idea waiting to emerge on how we Christians could get out of our churches to where people are.'

Well, it was not long before the idea did emerge. It was 'On the Move'. This book is all about the origins, development and literally the worldwide spread of this idea. It is a remarkable story, full of interventions from God, miracles of guidance, provision and indeed rescue in the context of cliff-edge situations. Repeatedly, all is risked towards the fulfillment of a very clear calling.

The risks were worth taking because something of

importance was being born. One of the characteristics of a really brilliant new idea is its simplicity. On the Move is a striking example of this. It reaches people in the open air with an attractive flavour of God's love for them. It provides a convivial atmosphere for meeting and eating. It makes people ask themselves, 'Is there such a thing as a free lunch after all? What makes these people so generous when I have done nothing to earn it?' And that, of course, is the question that makes people open to reflect on the good news of the gospel which is all about the free generosity of God to people who don't deserve it one little bit. These meals embody something of the grace of God—they are free of charge. The medium and the message point in the same direction. And it seems to work in every culture!

Many people respond at these outdoor meals. Some have burdens that they want one of the team to pray for. Some return to the Christian roots they have long abandoned. Some come to trust Christ for the first time, and get linked up with some church or organisation in the area where they live so that this first beginning of discipleship can be developed.

I confess that the first time I joined in an event put on by On the Move, I was quite willing to make a fool of myself by singing hymns in a group on the street. I was even willing to invite strangers to the lunch. But in my heart of hearts I was very doubtful whether anyone would come. Imagine my surprise when I came to the designated lunch area and found a long line of people waiting. It was wonderful to see how happy and amazed the guests were and how ready they were to discuss the Christian faith—and, for some of them, to commit themselves to Christian discipleship. That day I realised that an idea had been born whose time had come, and that it would grow. Now it has grown, literally worldwide. Read on, and be encouraged.

Michael Green

Part 1

1

The Crisis of the Moment

(Written on a flight from London to Tokyo, January 2004)

I am on a plane – on the first of the most important set of journeys of my life, taking me all over the world, launching a big vision I believe to be from God. I am also, as it happens, in the middle of the most dangerous and frightening crisis I have ever faced. The day before yesterday, I found out I have cancer.

And it is on this day – on the first of these flights – that I had planned to start writing my book. I even bought a laptop for the purpose. So here we are, in unpropitious circumstances, to say the least. But I do feel that maybe I should begin the book in any case. What a moment to start writing 'my story'!

*　　*　　*

Let's start with a bit more explanation. First, the 'vision' bit. It's Thursday the 29th January 2004 – two years before the likely publication of this book, the delay in publication being because the book is meant to culminate in something yet to happen. What is due to happen in 2005 is, effectively, an unprecedented world evangelistic mission.

Not that what we do is a big deal in itself. We do free barbecues with biggish teams of ordinary Christians from local churches working together. We take to the streets with several worship bands and a carnival atmosphere and invite all passers-by to the free barbecue. Hundreds come each day and God seems to touch many people, as church members host them, listen to them and pray for their needs. It's about as simple as the wheel . . . and it does seem to go places!

The plan for 2005 is for a co-ordinated outreach, in the power of the Holy Spirit, across the 30 main capital cities of the world. It seems incredible that the churches in all these cities would agree to such a thing, but I do believe that the idea is of God, in which case surely it can happen. It would be an unprecedented demonstration that there is *one church* throughout the world – the body of Christ – and that we can act as one, turn outwards to bless our communities and see God move, as we move as one. The signs have been very positive as we have sought to make contact with church leaders in distant lands. . .

So where are we flying? Japan first. Over ten days, four of us – our colleagues David and Barbara, my wife Gina and myself – will visit Tokyo, then Seoul and finally Beijing. We will meet church leaders and share the vision with them. Then we have tickets to visit Cairo, Jerusalem and Istanbul after a break of just five days; and then, after another five-day break, to visit Ottawa, Washington DC and Mexico City. We hope to visit 27 countries this year (having visited three in the course of 2003). That's if we get invited. Then, in

2005, the idea is that we return to all these countries (assuming they've agreed to have us!) one by one to do evangelistic missions, mobilising the local churches – all denominations working together – and taking to the streets with teams of hundreds of ordinary Christians. Or at least, that's the vision.

*   *   *

Now for the tricky bit. I don't know if I'll be able to make the trips to the Middle East and North America, though the tickets are already bought – or any of the trips after that. This whole vision could be stillborn. Will I be well enough to see it through? Will I be alive?

Normally, you read 'happy ever after' books, which were written knowing the outcome. This is not the case here. The book is being started – this first chapter is being written – two days after I was diagnosed as having cancer, in my mouth of all places.

Here's how we found out. I was travelling with Gina eleven days ago to the town of Farnham, in Surrey, to give five-minute presentations in six churches in one morning. That's the sort of schedule I've followed most Sundays between January and June for the last six years. I must have spoken in 500 churches (and our little organisation as a whole has done presentations in 1,500) in that time. On this occasion, we were to come away with the names and addresses of 220 people who volunteered that morning to take part in an On the Move mission in a few months' time – a normal Sunday morning 'haul'. But on the way there, as we travelled eastwards in the car with the morning sun shining into my face, I put down the visor. Looking in the mirror on the back of the visor, I found that with the sun shining directly from the front, I could see right into my mouth. So I started gawking at myself in the mirror (Gina was driving!).

Then I saw it. At the back of my mouth, hanging from the palate, was a big lump, the size of the end of my thumb. I started getting worried, but didn't know quite what to make of it. Gina was a tower of strength, but quietly worried too. I telephoned the doctor on Monday morning. She saw me at 2.00 p.m. that day and said that I was right to be anxious, as it could be cancer. I had thought of it, but didn't want to use that word.

I came home feeling shaken. I asked the Lord to give me an encouragement from Scripture. I didn't half need one. I had the number 112 fixed in my mind and so I looked up the psalm of that number, as I do when a number appears in my mind like that. The psalm was all about the righteous man 'who is not afraid of bad news'. That helped, but. . .

Some dear friends who had heard about my problem came round to pray that evening, and from that point (though not before) I did feel at peace. I seem to combine a very active mind, which is always thinking around every eventuality, with a sense of God's presence and an assurance that he will do it. This can make for peace and anxiety at the same time! So I do tend to need a supernatural peace to keep my mind quiet.

The doctor somehow managed to get me an appointment with the specialist for 9.30 the next morning – amazing, since this is the UK National Health Service, which isn't famed for doing things quickly. The specialist decided that I needed to see someone else and he called him on his mobile to see if he was in Birmingham. In response, we heard a loud knock on the wall. He was in the next room – and came in immediately. It turned out he had time to see me that day, because his main patient had been wrongly allocated to him and he had nothing else to do! He said it was a tumour of the minor salivary gland and that it might or might not be malignant. Not only did he see me: he got me a chest X-ray about two hours later, and about two hours after that, he did the operation!

Before I went into theatre, I felt the need for some more encouragement, so we looked at *The Times* Scripture verse, carried daily in the personal columns. On this day it said, 'Let Jesus Christ be as close to you as the clothes you are wearing' (from Romans 13). That is the verse that was on my mind as, minutes later, I was wheeled on a trolley to the operating theatre.

When I came to after the operation, I was told that most – but not all – of the tumour had been removed. I got the shock of my life later, at home, when I looked in the mirror. There was a crater the size of half a plum where the tumour had been.

I felt quite low and, frankly, unable to pray. I just wanted to be in 'receive mode'. So I asked the Lord to speak to me. The name 'Gideon' soon came into my mind. I was so hungry to hear from God and rapidly looked up Judges, to read about the call of Gideon. The angel of the Lord appears to him and says, 'The LORD is with you, mighty warrior.' Ten verses later (Judges 6:22), it says, 'When Gideon realised that it was the angel of the LORD, he exclaimed, "Ah, Sovereign LORD! I have seen the angel of the LORD face to face!"

But the LORD said to him, "Peace! Do not be afraid. You are not going to die."'

I was not going to die from this tumour. *I am not going to die* from it. I am sure that God spoke to me.

The next day, I had an MRI scan (for which there is normally a 15-month waiting list). The results from the scan and from the biopsy were due to be given on the following Tuesday – the day before yesterday.

Tuesday arrived. I was peaceful enough, though weak and still in considerable pain from the operation. Loads of people had been praying for me. Our whole church had prayed for Gina and myself on the Sunday evening. We had never felt so loved, though probably never so much in need of it.

The news went from bad to worse. It was a malignant tumour. And, while they had removed 98 per cent of it, the remaining 2 per cent was on the hard palate – the bone structure. They would have a case conference the next day (yesterday) to decide what to do.

Yesterday we heard – and it was yet worse than expected. They would need to do a really major operation – removing and reconstructing my palate with a thick skin graft from my left arm – and also radiotherapy. One side effect would be the serious impairment of my voice. I would speak in a wheezy and nasal voice and would need speech therapy, to learn to pronounce many ordinary words as well as possible. My salivary glands (and my taste buds) would also be killed, leaving me with a permanently dry mouth. These would seem to be death knells to a ministry based on public speaking. So my job and ministry are on the line, not to mention my life.

I told the consultant, very briefly, about the calling I felt I had received and about our travel plans, starting in two days. He received this very positively (I described myself as one of these mad people who believe that God speaks to them!) and he promised to do what he could to work around our travel dates. The following day he confirmed that it would be OK for me to go to the Far East and he would see me on my return from the first trip.

*   *   *

That was yesterday. So was the dinner in London. Months ago, we had organised for me to do a presentation about the international vision to an invited audience of about 60 in a nice hotel. Two thirds of them were church leaders from 14 areas of London where we had done missions (and so this was effectively the launch of a London mission for 2005 as part of the 30 capitals programme). The other third were Christian businesspeople, with a view to fundraising. But, after months of planning, my emergency operation seemed on the brink of ruining it all. The night before the presentation it still hurt me to speak at all. Was I going to be able to speak at the dinner? All this was on a wing and a prayer, and not much of a wing at that!

Yesterday morning, it snowed. Everything was in chaos (a great British tradition when it snows) and it took us two hours just to get out of Birmingham (instead of the normal 15 minutes). The journey remained agonisingly slow: we arrived in London an hour and a half late for our own dinner.

Somehow, my voice 'worked', for the first time since the

operation. I spoke, in fact, for three quarters of an hour. At the end, I told them in full about the cancer. People were moved. They received the vision wonderfully – and sent us off to Japan.

So here we are, on the plane. If you're still reading this, don't be downcast. I don't take to tragedies either! And I know that my God can get me out of any fix. He has done so many times. I do firmly believe (mad though it may seem) that this book will have the happiest of endings – all the happier for the 'many dangers, toils and snares' come through along the way. And you can't have a cliffhanger without the cliff.

I don't know where it's all going to lead. I do feel strangely confident in my heart that the missions in 2005 will in fact happen. But I don't know how God will do it.

To be honest, I *am* scared. I do at the same time carry a strong sense of destiny about what we are doing. And I feel safe in God's hands. All three at once!

I hope and pray that after reading our story so far, and up to the end of 2005, *your* faith will be greatly encouraged. We have regularly seen God move in quite remarkable ways, and I choose to think that we are in the middle of the most remarkable episode of all. I want you to have such a faith that you can face disaster and still know faith – and come through the other end victorious. I think that this attack on my health is just that, an attack, and it comes solely because what God is doing is big. I believe we will have the victory in this. I believe! It's something I want to be able to impart to you, the reader. This is for you too.

I hope you find this journey exciting as you come with us, starting at the beginning. It has been a roller-coaster ride so far and it doesn't look much like ceasing to be one at this point! But I trust that you will be inspired about the kind of relationship you can have with the Lord as you believe and step out – and about the kind of fruit that can flow from it.

We have had fun and excitement (when Gina became a Christian her 'condition' to God was that he would make her life exciting. . .), and we have had immense challenges. This account will be real, as I so much want you in your own life to embark on a journey of faith, or remain on it if you are already on such a journey – but I also want to be able to guide you (through our story) concerning some of the things you might expect and some of the things we are learning. For example, not everything seems to happen in a straight line. There are some blind alleys along the way. One discerns the hand of God in some of them afterwards – very clearly! And you need to walk through the minefield with faith, but also with your eyes open, operating in the guidance and discernment of the Holy Spirit. It's a battle for which we can receive training.

It's like a dance you can learn. The Lord is a forgiving partner, when you step on his feet trying!

2

The Calling

That first chapter was written well before the denouement – the events of our 'big year' of 2005. Now, as I introduce the rest of this book, and with the benefit of hindsight, I happen to know the end! I am, I can tell you, still alive. All of what follows was written on plane journeys (111 of them) during 2004 and 2005. Missions indeed took place in capital cities all over the world. Amazing things happened and amazing things are flowing from what was begun. It is as if a 'yeast' was added to the mixture of the church around the world, and something new is rising.

But every story has a start. Every journey with God begins with something, somehow, breaking into ordinary lives and starting a process of transformation. This is how God did it in our case; this is how he then carried us on eagles' wings, and how we hung on with increasing amazement to see the extent of the ground covered – and the breathtaking view which has since opened up.

*   *   *

It wasn't always like this – the relatively comfortable life I was enjoying in 1995, the good job, the prominence (on a local level at least), the relative prosperity. Everything had been so different when Gina and I got married in 1980, and then a few years later when the Christian rock band we'd put so much love and effort into collapsed. Then we didn't have two pennies to rub together. There was much optimism, to be sure, as we made it our business to seek God, to *prove* in our lives that one could step out in faith and see him act. Our commitment had been to *hear* God too, and what we felt we heard had led us to take risks. I remember the one winter when we almost froze, with the one gas fire burning our fronts, while the bare draughty cold of our open-plan house froze the rest of us. All because we had started to reshape our house, but hadn't yet found the money to complete it!

We had placed much hope in the band, which failed; subsequently we started a salad business, which plateaued at a level not good enough to live on, so we jacked that in. As for my academic studies at Cambridge which were to have led to a PhD, that failed too when I was given an MLitt (a sort of poor man's PhD) after my thesis got stuck in a range war between the vice chancellor, who thought it was excellent, and some others who favoured a newer way of doing political philosophy. So, my life had looked to be in quite a mess.

And that doesn't sit easily with a fractured identity, born of family trauma. My German Jewish parents had fled the Nazis in the 1930s, my father's brother having quite separately come to grief in Russia and been executed in one of Stalin's purges (and then later 'rehabilitated'). Subsequently my father, by 1950 a successful physician in America, lost his job there because he had been deemed a 'security risk' in the McCarthy era, apparently because his uncle had been a socialist leader back in Germany (in opposition to the Nazis) and this somehow made my dad a 'communist'.

So when *they* made good and attained senior positions in medicine (my dad) and academia (my mum), there was a sense that this is something you don't lose.

Yet Gina and I wanted to see the life of real healings, real guidance, real trust in God that we witnessed in the Scriptures, being acted out in our lives. This must involve risk.

When you ask God to move in your life, to prune you, to stretch you, to 'take you places', you embark on a journey of which you are not the author. In many instances, the choice is between hanging on or getting off. But, in so far as you hang on, you become totally dependent on the God you are learning to trust. It's a walk that will prove your faith – or otherwise. This makes life exciting, but also daunting. Faith is no longer a theory or a feeling. It's a basis for making decisions that may run directly counter to the ones you would normally make, because you believe that God is telling you to do so, and because you love him.

What is life like, when you embark on such a journey? That's what this book is about – the highs and the lows, the thrill and the fulfilment that comes from taking your feet off the ground and learning to walk by the Spirit.

*   *   *

I met Gina (or, rather, almost met her) at my rock band's biggest concert, in February 1978, with an audience of over

600 celebrating the tenth anniversary of Tearfund. I sat in the audience in the first half – my band being scheduled to top the bill in the second half. Behind me sat Gina. She is from Nicaragua, in Central America, and she had asked her father to send her to England to join her sister, who was learning English. The idea was to go back to complete her medical studies in Mexico (she had done three years) after a gap year in Cambridge. It was not to be. . .

She turned to her sister at this concert in the Guildhall to discuss the young man (me) sitting in front of her, whom she apparently found very attractive. (It has to be said that she is, to this day, short-sighted.) She resolved to ask me where I got my can of Coke as a way of opening a conversation. Then she noticed that I was sitting next to a woman and a child and wrongly deduced that I must be married. Then, in the second half of the concert, she saw me up front with the band.

But that was that. She soon walked out of the concert (being unimpressed by the band and not liking rock music in any case). So much for the young man sitting in front of her.

During the next few days, Gina had to find new accommodation, as her landlady needed the room for her own daughter. She put out feelers at a party and a student told her that the house where he lived had a spare room. He promised to ask the owner whether Gina could come and stay for twelve days. Well, the owner of that house was me. I asked the student whether this girl was nice. He said that she seemed to be, and so I said, 'OK then.'

Gina arrived – a strikingly attractive and vivacious young lady from Latin America. She immediately recognised me as the person she had fancied about ten days before at the concert. She told me she had seen me there. I asked her if she had enjoyed it. She replied, 'It was wonderful!'

Gina and I started going out – and then she moved out. After nine months I proposed, and luckily she said 'yes'.

We got married nine months after that. It was a moving wedding – certainly for us, but for others too. At the bit where we had to say our vows, Gina was overcome with emotion, not least because her parents weren't able to be there. She couldn't speak. The Revd Sidney Sims suggested that he would say the vows and she could simply say 'Amen'. This she did just manage, much to my relief – and long-term benefit, as I can remind her of the 'Amen' whenever she mentions, at moments of tactical manoeuvring, that she didn't actually say her vows!

*   *   *

In our married life, the first crunch came when the Lord started telling us to trust him financially. This can be a crunch issue for many people and there is no doubt that it is capable of challenging one to the core. We were on a derisory income, but in faith we started taking big risks in that area. What happened? Things just got worse! Eventually we hit rock bottom and the bank withdrew our cards and froze our account. It was *then* that we started to see God act.

Then started an extraordinary period of divine provision. A French friend who was staying with us at the time couldn't believe what he saw. And nor, very nearly, could we. Money would come through the letterbox – five pounds here, ten pounds there. Once Gina rushed to the door to see who it was who had just posted some money through. Looking along the terraced street to the right and the left, she saw that the street was empty. Yet there was nowhere to hide.

It was interesting how this miraculous provision didn't start until it was really needed. But now that it *was* really needed, it really started. We needed £51.70 for a telephone bill. We prayed for the money to pay it. Finally, very late in the day, a cheque for £52 arrived in the post. We walked to the payment centre to pay our bill. On arriving home, we found that the telephone had just been cut off. So we returned to the centre, able to say that we had *already paid the bill*. We were immediately reinstated, amidst profuse apologies.

On one occasion, we ordered a new carpet by faith, because we were so convinced that God had said we should. When the carpet-fitters arrived to lay it, we were £27 short of the sum needed to pay for it. Amazingly, the fitters announced on their arrival that the underlay had just come on offer and that they would do it for us at the lower price. Who makes a sale at one price and *then* reduces it? But that's exactly what they did. Yet we were still £5 short. What were we going to do? How would we tell the fitters that we were unable to pay the full amount? Just as the fitters were finishing up, our friend Jonathan cycled up to the house, announcing that he had come to return £5 that he had borrowed from us some time before, because he had a strong sense from the Lord that he must bring it to us now!

Another time my mother phoned and said that she and

my father would, if that were OK, come and see us for dinner on the Saturday and, by the way, could she have boiled
chicken, as her stomach was feeling delicate. (You should
have seen her pill drawer!) Of course I said that was fine,
and then we pondered the fact that there was no money to
buy this chicken for the next day – and we definitely didn't
want my parents to know about the situation in which we
had found ourselves. The key thing, we felt, was to trust the
Lord and to be obedient to his word that we should rely on
him. Naive stuff! But sometimes there is a great power in
naivety.

Saturday morning came and, to our disappointment,
there was no cheque in the post, nor any mysterious fivers
through the letterbox. The afternoon rolled on. In those
days the shops closed at 5.30 prompt on a Saturday evening
and that would be that. Our good friend Louise was due to
pop in at about 4.00 p.m. and we agreed that we would ask
her to lend us £5. She came – and went. Gina and I had both
independently felt restrained from asking for the loan.

Now, at nearly 5.00 p.m., I was getting desperate. I said,
'Lord, you have to do something, and now!' I immediately
had in my mind a picture of a £10 note. Somehow, it was
clear to me that this £10 note was *in the house* and I needed
to find it. The first place I thought to look in was my jacket
pockets in the wardrobe. First jacket, nothing. Second
jacket, in the right-hand pocket, a sealed but unmarked air-
mail envelope. I brought it downstairs and said to Gina, 'Do
you know what this is?' She didn't. So, with some trepidation, we opened it. Inside we found two £10 notes.

I wonder whether I have ever experienced such a sense
of joy, of elation. It wasn't just the money. It was the direct

confirmation to us that God was *real*, that he was *close* and *there for us*; that the picture of the £10 note had really been from him; that he could rescue us in a crisis. What a moment!

So we went to the shops and bought the chicken, plus ice cream, plus wine, plus God knows what else. At any rate, the money was spent and my parents were received royally that evening.

Those were wonderful times. There are so many examples of God's provision and faithfulness. Our home was a house of prayer. These were exciting days and the excitement was infectious. One or two people got healed. God often spoke to us. There was a tremendous sense of anticipation.

*   *   *

Then it all started to clear up. I got a decent job, which led to a better one (as public affairs director of the British Chambers of Commerce); then a better one, this time in national politics (as the number two in the Conservative Research Department, where I wrote key publications, speeches, articles and the like, and was on course to become an MP); and then as chief executive of the Kent Chamber of Commerce and Industry. And while we looked back with fondness at the time when we saw the Lord move in our lives, there was also a bit of a sense of 'never again'. It had been hard, even while exhilarating. We now had four children (aged between five and twelve in 1995) and a sizeable detached house (with an equally sizeable mortgage) in a pretty village in Kent; we had a dog, a cat and a goldfish;

and my work was going brilliantly. Work was itself exciting, and not without its challenges.

But something, by that year, had changed again. Neither Gina nor I were satisfied. Having for years intended to go into politics, I now said I no longer felt my heart was in it (this set Gina praying, hard). Life was somehow empty – *boring*, actually. We wanted to see God glorified in our lives. We were once again thirsty to see God *move*. We actually became desperate for this to happen.

*   *   *

It was into this situation that God spoke. I was sitting in my church, not-listening to the sermon, when it happened. I suddenly 'realised' that I was to go into full-time Christian ministry. In spite of all I have just said, this was actually a complete surprise. I was looking for God to move: I wasn't remotely expecting a career change.

The service ended about ten minutes after this (for me) dramatic realisation. It had suddenly seemed obvious that full-time Christian ministry was what I was *always* going to do. As I pondered this, and wondered what to make of it, the lady sitting directly behind me (whom I didn't know) tapped me on the shoulder and said, 'Excuse me, but during the sermon I felt God saying that *it's time for you to be released into your ministry.*'

What a bombshell! I was trying to deal with this new happening when, moments later, Gina came up to me and added her piece to the equation. She said, 'During the sermon, I felt the Lord showing me things about your future, but I'm not going to tell you until he shows you.' (She's like that – awkward!)

I asked her, 'Is it that I'm to go into full-time Christian ministry?'

'Yes!'

The Lord had actually come to Gina with a question: 'Would you be willing to release Martin to serve me?' There had been something of a running joke in our household that, should I ever go into Christian ministry, she would pack her bags and 'go back to Nicaragua'. Now, in this new light, she quickly assessed her life and concluded that there was no future in opposing God. She said to the Lord, 'Yes, but you'll have to show him. I won't lift a finger to tell him.' All this happened as I was receiving my own revelation, and then immediately hearing it confirmed by the stranger in the row behind. Three ways in the same 15 minutes! That was compelling. God was making himself very, very clear.

A week after this, at the end of May 1995, we were in Canada. We had been booked to go to the church in Toronto that all the publicity had been about. We had wanted to check out the 'Toronto Blessing', a brand-new phenomenon at that time. Indeed, it was Gina who was so adamant that we should go, as she wanted more of the Lord. Then, when she'd had a vision of ourselves on a plane with a number of individuals we knew, going to Toronto, I was persuaded that the Lord was telling us to go.

We loved what we saw at the Airport church and, one evening when Paul Cain was leading a time of ministry, he asked, 'Would those who feel called to evangelism please stand up? I want to pray for you.' I guess a couple of hundred of the 2,000 people there stood up, including myself. Why did I stand? Well, it was most interesting. I experienced a *purely physical* impulse to stand. I *had* to stand,

and only in doing so did I draw the conclusion that evangelism must be a key part of the content of my calling.

We made a couple of friends who were members of the church there and they invited us back for what turned out to be an utterly hilarious lunch, with the jerky movements associated with the 'Toronto Blessing' causing our host to send forkfuls of spaghetti all over the place, the dining room ceiling included. But the most significant moment (even for a spaghetti lover like me) came when we turned to prayer and one of their other guests had a prophetic word for me. This lady said that she could see God putting on my feet a pair of seven-league boots. (Did I know the children's story about the man who had these and could take huge steps whenever he put them on?) God, she saw, was giving me seven-league boots 'and the Lord will cause you to take great big steps for the kingdom of God'.

This produced more hilarity. But what was I to do now? I had an apparent calling – something about evangelism and something about big steps – which I had not a clue how to fulfil.

*   *   *

We conferred with a number of people. The general sense was that this was indeed a call from God. One key piece of advice was from a friend who said that, if you didn't know how to fulfil a call, the best thing was to do nothing. Otherwise you risked doing what Abraham did: he received a call referring to Isaac, and jumped the gun with his servant, producing Ishmael and a massive number of problems further down the line. Better to wait for God to fulfil the promise he had made, in his own way and in his own time.

So we waited. Surely God had a plan. Surely he could get me there.

I didn't have to wait long. One person we had already met, John Collins, former vicar of Holy Trinity Brompton and very much an evangelist, had felt that I should *do* some evangelism. He wrote to Michael Green to see if he could help in taking me under his wing. In October 1995 (the calling had been in May), I received a letter from Michael suggesting that I might take a week off the following March to join him in Bolton as part of a team for a mission he was leading there. It was a Springboard mission (Springboard being the current Archbishops' initiative for evangelism) and he also suggested that, while I was at it, I should meet Martin Cavender, Springboard director, who was also in Kent, based in the precincts of Canterbury Cathedral.

I contacted Martin and he ended up coming round for lunch in early December 1995. How does God set about opening doors? Here is an example. Martin and I got on like a house on fire and, in the course of the conversation, I said to him, 'By the way, I'm good at fundraising.' Martin immediately spilt the beans. He confessed to Gina and me that he had been with Archbishop George Carey the previous day and had presented him with the names of about 15 people whom he was proposing to ask to join a new 'executive council' for Springboard. The list included four bishops, Michael Green, Viscountess Brentford and others of a similar calibre – 'the great and the good', as they say. The Archbishop had approved the people on the list being approached, but added that Martin also needed to find someone who was 'gifted at fundraising'. And so it was that, on his way to seeing me the following day, he had laid out a fleece, saying in his prayers, 'If this Martin Graham, who is a businessman, is possibly the one, *let him say that he has a gift for fundraising.*' Which I duly did! About a month later, I received a letter from Archbishop George Carey asking me to join this executive council. I thought this was actually quite funny, since I had little experience in evangelism and no contacts or 'profile' whatsoever in the wider church. If God could cause such a person to be invited by the Archbishop of Canterbury to join this top council 'out of nothing', then he could surely do anything.

One other thing had happened a couple of days before I met Martin. I had been to a weekend Christian conference of about 80 people, led by Ian Andrews. Our friend Louise had intended to go with her daughter, who had dropped out at the last moment. Louise thought it might do me good to go.

Before I went, talking and praying with Gina, we 'negotiated' (as it were) with God the things we wanted him to clarify for us. These boiled down to three questions, clearly formulated at the time.

(1) 'Is this calling really from you, Lord, or is it our imagination?' Following the apparent blind alley that had been the Christian rock band in which I had genuinely felt called to play lead guitar for years until 1985, we needed to know.

(2) 'If so, how is it going to work financially?' We had a big mortgage and four children, all of which needed to be supported – by me. Particularly with the children at the kinds of ages they were, I had clear responsibilities.

(3) 'Will I enjoy evangelism?' I had no particular convic-
    tion that evangelism was what I *wanted* to do, or evi-
    dence – for that matter – that it was something I would
    be any good at.

The conference was in full swing on the Saturday when Ian
Andrews said he had a 'picture' of a wandering minstrel. He
said to the guitarist that he believed God was saying that he
should *sing* prophecies to people. The guitarist (a braver
man than I) started out. He went up to one person in the
audience and, guitar in hand, sang an improvised song,
which was in the form of a personal prophecy from God to
that person. Then came another; then another. The songs
were both beautiful and fluent. Some of them, remarkably,
came out in rhyme. Then, before he could get to me, it was
time for the tea break! Those infernal English. . .

I *knew* God had something for me and was praying hard
during tea, and as we resumed the meeting Ian (thankfully)
said that the personal prophecies should continue – and the
guitarist turned to me.

Now I should stress that no-one at the meeting save for
Louise knew about the calling I had received. The guitarist
didn't know me from Adam (nor I him). What follows is
an exact transcript of what was sung, and then said. I can
do this verbatim because the meeting was recorded and I
purchased a copy of the tape. I only wish the lovely tune
could be incorporated into this transcript. As you read it,
bear in mind our three questions: was the calling our
imagination, how would it work financially, and would I
enjoy it?

I have called you, Martin
[The 'Martin' bit wasn't a miracle: I was wearing a name badge!]
It's my voice you have heard
The answer to your question is 'yes', my son
The answer to your heart-cry is 'now', dear son
Martin I have called you to my heart's desire
Martin I have set before you my heart's desire
Don't think that it's your imagination
Don't think that it's just a dream
Don't think that it won't happen
Or you won't get paid
[On the tape you can hear the sound of laughter here]

Martin I have called you
I have set my seal upon you
Martin I have made a way in the wilderness
There's no thing that I can't do for you
There's no mountain I won't move
For you are my beloved
And you please me more than you know
You are my beloved son

So don't look at the circumstances
And don't say it can't be done
Just look up to my lovely face
And you will find all the grace that you need

I will make a way for you, son
Where there has been no way
You won't find another who is walking
In the way that I make you walk
For you are a mould-breaker
And you are one of a kind
Yes you are a mould-breaker

And you are one of a kind
And the miracles will happen
And the miracles will happen
Yes the miracles will happen
As you trust me

Step out of your past, step out of your family
Step out of your past, step out of your history
Today is the day of your salvation
You were born for a day like this
You were born for a ministry like this

And you will like what I do
More than you liked the former thing
You will like what I do
And you will stand out in my kingdom
You will like what I do
For I have called you to shine for me
[Here the tape was turned over and something may have been lost]
Who do you think it came from
Your hopes for ministry?
From me, from me, my beloved.

[Now spoken, not sung]
The Lord says, 'Martin, double it, double it
Whatever you are asking for, double it
They're not big enough – your requests are not big enough
Your prayers for the sick are not big enough
Your request for finance is not big enough
Your desires for your own time and your own life are not
    big enough
Double it, double the things you are asking.'

It's a bit like Solomon, where the Lord has seen what you have
not asked for and wants to give you these things. Because you

have not asked for fame and wealth and all these things, the Lord is going to make a way; the Lord is going to make a way.

The guitarist then asked the audience to pray for me, saying, 'Something amazing is happening here. I don't really understand it; I just know that it's amazing.'

After I had been prayed for, I was invited to the microphone and was able to explain about the calling I had received six months earlier. I said I didn't know what it was about exactly, but was trusting the Lord.

I really can say that after that moment, I never doubted the call I'd received. I telephoned Gina shortly afterwards in great excitement and said, 'You'll never guess what just happened. . .' All three questions had been answered, with extraordinary directness. It was quite thrilling. Imagine, too, the sense of relief that floods into a pretty insecure situation: God is on my case; he is speaking directly to me; I can trust him. I must trust him.

But how would he actually do it?

*   *   *

The following March, I went to join Michael Green and his team in Bolton. Michael was very welcoming and appreciative and I started joining in as best I could. I prepared various talks and was essentially posted to home meetings, where someone from one of the churches might have invited four or five neighbours around to hear the 'guest speaker'. I did several of these and enjoyed them immensely – and found out that it *was* 'me', incorporating many aspects of who I am, not least my love for music.

Then came one of God's 'incidents' – and the key moment (for me) of the mission. There was a business breakfast with about 50 invited guests present and Michael Green was to give the main talk. I was asked to go in support since, as chief executive of the Kent Chamber of Commerce, I could add the 'business' element to the platform.

Michael sketched out to me the structure of the morning. As the businessman, I was to do about ten minutes of welcome. Then he would do another ten minutes or so, setting out his theme for the morning. Then it would be over to me again to add what I wanted to. Finally, he would finish up.

So I did the welcome bit and then Michael started speaking. He spoke ever so well and I noticed what I would now call 'the anointing' on certain words and challenges he was offering. It was as if there was something going out of him at that point. Then it was my turn. The problem was that Michael had spoken for over 40 minutes and it was now 9.20 a.m. I know a business audience and, come 9.30, someone will get up to leave and then immediately another half dozen will go and one begins to lose it. It was just the circumstances of the moment that drove me to it. As Michael was finishing his talk, I wrote him a brief note saying that I really felt we needed to finish by 9.30 and, if it was all right with him, I would pull the strands together and conclude the meeting. As it happens, he didn't see the note until later. . .

So I got up and said a bit more about the gospel and then said that I hoped it didn't seem totally inappropriate to pray at a business seminar, but there might be people who would like to 'connect' with the God that had made them and that I would pray a prayer which they could quietly pray with me if they would like to. I did this and there certainly seemed to be a Holy Spirit moment as I led the prayer. I then sat down.

It was only as Michael made some concluding remarks that I realised what I had done. I had nicked the altar call from a famous evangelist! *Nobody does that.*

Michael was graciousness itself and was immensely encouraging about what he had heard me do. From that moment, amazingly, I had a friend.

*   *   *

Skip forward three months to the end of June 1996. Gina and I were house group leaders. In fact, one of the immediate apparent fruits of the calling was that we were invited, quite coincidentally, to take up various kinds of leadership. We turned up one Thursday at the house group and Gina's opening gambit to the ten of us there was to ask, with her winning smile, 'Shall I drop the bomb now?' All of us, including myself, looked at her. What was coming next?

I should stress here that Gina has been strongly prophetic for as long as I have known her. Indeed, as a 14-year-old in Nicaragua, she had become involved in the Catholic charismatic movement and God had given her pictures, dreams and prophetic words and caused her to take steps of faith then – not least the one that got her father a job after Gina felt she should approach a Christian millionaire in a conference of 10,000 people. She had said, 'Lord, I will ask him *if* you place him, with his wife, sitting directly behind me in this lonely chapel right now, so that he's there when I look around.' After quite a while of trying to pluck up courage, she did turn around – and there they were, the man and his wife, in the seats directly behind her.

Now, ahead of our house group meeting, she had been fasting and had received a vision in which she clearly heard the Lord say that there should be an evangelistic mission in Harrietsham, the next village along from ours; that our house group should lead the mission; and that it should take place in the first weekend in August, seven weeks hence.

We all tried to take in what was indeed a bombshell. The next surprise was that everyone actually loved the idea – not remotely typical of ten Anglicans being told that they were to lead an evangelistic mission, having never done so before in their lives.

I asked who would actually be available in the first weekend of August, it being holiday time. Everyone, without exception, was available. In addition, we happened to know the rector of the church in Harrietsham. Where from? Well, we had met him in Toronto, when I had turned to the elderly man sitting next to me amongst 2,000 people in the Airport Church and asked, 'Where are you from?' Imagine our surprise when it turned out to be England, then Kent, then Harrietsham, the neighbouring village. . .

So Gina contacted the rector, Revd Alan Stockbridge, and asked what he thought of the idea. He *loved* it. He was finishing his first Alpha course in the last week of July and had been praying for something to follow it. A mission over the first weekend of August would be ideal.

We met his outreach committee, a good-hearted lot, who put their caution aside and let this untried group lead their first ever mission. Again, highly unusual.

The format of the mission that we chose echoed the Springboard home meetings scenario and all members of the house group gave a talk or a testimony – and God certainly blessed it. Then we had a youth event (fairly thinly attended), a family fun day and then, lo and behold, a barbecue in the rectory garden. This was done through personally written invitations to parishioners, and about 120 came. It was a wonderful evening and a number of people gave their lives to Christ.

I now felt the Lord saying that I should gather a team of 50 people from our church (of about 400) who would be willing to do this kind of mission. Our vicar agreed. Gina and I wrote down the names of the people we felt we should approach. In no time at all, we had 50.

The idea of mobilising ordinary Christians had a slightly earlier genesis within me. At the Bolton mission I'd had a delightful evening with Michael and Rosemary Green in which I formulated my emerging view that Springboard should change tack. I felt the mission was very good as far as it went. People were touched and lives were changed. But after local church members had been caught up in the 'spirit of mission', the show left town, leaving them – in a sense – high and dry. They were marched up the hill, and then marched down again. The key thing was to mobilise the ordinary Christians for mission – and keep them mobilised. Maybe a membership scheme?

In any case, we had our 50 ready in our own church to be used for mission. They were needed much sooner than we had anticipated – all of them.

3

Canterbury

The Springboard office asked me to meet someone in Canterbury. He was an American Episcopalian priest named Jon Shuler, who said he had years before received a vision to lead an evangelistic mission to Canterbury in May 1997. He wanted to meet community leaders and, because I was a Christian and ran the Kent Chamber, someone at the Springboard office thought that I would do. So I agreed to come to Canterbury to meet him in December 1996, really as a favour to Springboard.

The person I met was smallish, engaging and highly likeable. He told me how he had been walking down the streets of Canterbury in 1991 when he had been transported in a vision. He 'saw' a mission happening on the streets of Canterbury and he knew that it was to take place in 1997 to coincide with the 1,400th anniversary of St Augustine arriving in Canterbury from Rome in 597 to bring the gospel to England. Some 10,000 had been baptised in one week in a mighty move of God, and Canterbury (St Augustine's base) became the spiritual centre of this work – and of what was one day to become the Church of England.

Hundreds of years later, the gospel had been taken from Canterbury (as it were) to much of the world. Now, in 1997, this missionary moment was being marked; but, in typically Anglican style, it was to be celebrated with trumpets in Canterbury Cathedral, a visit from Prince Charles, and other commemorative acts – but no mission! It took an American to put forward the proposal that there should be an evangelistic mission.

I met Jon at the end of 1996 and I did feel that the vision he brought was from God. I also shared with him what we had done in Harrietsham, based on a vision – and a very short timescale of seven weeks to fulfil it. He was encouraged. Apart from some mutual encouragement, nothing much happened. I was struck, however, by the picture he described to me, whereby he had seen an 'arc of fire' landing in Canterbury and producing an explosion. This explosion had sent other arcs of fire springing out in several directions at once. Each one then landed in another town or city, producing another explosion, which in turn sent further arcs of fire spreading in all directions. A very striking vision.

I met Jon again in February of 1997. He was back in Kent and this time he had found his way to my own church, not because he knew I was there, but because someone had suggested he should get in touch with my vicar, Eric Delve. Before the service started, Eric came up to me and said, 'There's someone I want you to meet.' Jon and I greeted each other warmly. When Jon was invited to share his vision later in the service, he finished up by saying that, if anyone wanted to get involved, they should speak to Martin! He apologised afterwards for dropping me in it.

Later, Gina and I prayed together and, in a message in tongues and interpretation, we believed we heard God telling us: 'I want you to devote yourselves to this mission.' So it was that, not long afterwards, I telephoned Jon in the United States and offered to help. I was immediately appointed 'UK co-ordinator' of the Canterbury mission!

Not for the first (or last) time, a message in tongues and interpretation was to prove crucial. Gina and I started on that track shortly after we married. We were reading from Genesis, about Abraham bargaining with God about whether he would still destroy Sodom and Gomorrah if there were 50 righteous men, then 40, 30, and so on. Each time God relented. But what fascinated us was the *conversation*. If Abraham could talk to God like that, *and get an answer*, why couldn't we? We resolved that we could and would – and subsequently did! These things are by faith (and the Bible and the episodes recorded there are potentially such releasers of faith for the things we *don't* see). Our prayer times together became crucial. Gina would often give a message in tongues. What is clear when such a message is given is that the person with the 'interpretation' receives something at that moment that simply wasn't there before the tongue was given. Indeed, when Gina gives a tongue, I feel something coming upon me – rather like the feeling of oil being poured on my head, and of a beautiful sort of 'pregnancy' rising inside – and words start welling up, which I then try to speak out faithfully.

I have two thoughts here. First, when husband and wife pray together, something so powerful is released it's no wonder that one of Satan's most effective devices is to make it feel to many couples *so difficult* to pray together. Don't be put off: go through the pain barrier and do it. There will be rich rewards. Second, hearing God speak is of seminal importance, again and again. He has the words of eternal life. Hearing those words, spoken specifically to us, has changed everything, repeatedly.

It certainly did this time. God had told us to help Jon Shuler. I was now his UK co-ordinator. Jon flew over again to discuss what we would do.

This was the situation. There was no local church support in Canterbury. In fact, the Anglican churches had written Jon a letter, penned with that peculiarly English indirectness, which others had to inform Jon meant 'Go away!' Yet Jon and 40 Americans, who had all caught the vision and were paying their own airfares, had finally said 'We're coming anyway', so convinced were they that this was a call from God.

Second, there was no format for the mission. There was no conception of what the 40 Americans, or anyone else for that matter, would actually *do* during the mission. All that was in place was the dates. The Americans would arrive on the 22nd May. The mission would start on the 26th May (the key anniversary) and would continue until the 8th June. That was about it. Oh, and there was no money.

One more thing. The 26th May was just seven weeks away. . .

So, in the absence of any discernible plan, Gina, Jon and I settled down in our living room to pray. We asked the Lord to show us what to do.

As we prayed, I had a clear image in my mind of a loaf of bread. I looked up and said, 'I think the Lord wants us to *feed* people.' Jon went somewhat green at the thought of all the administration involved in feeding the masses as I sketched out a possible plan, but he accepted it as from the Lord. Basically the idea was that we should have a free barbecue every day in the local park, somewhere near the high street shopping area. Some team members would prepare the food. Meanwhile, others would form worship bands and occupy prominent positions in the high street. Still other team members would go up to the passers-by and say, 'Can I invite you to a free barbecue?' A fourth group would act as hosts at the tables, welcoming our guests to the barbecue and speaking with them and ministering to them in prayer. That was it.

There was a lot we didn't know about what we would do: whether it would work and, if so, how it would work, and – for that matter – *why* it would work. But, walking on the water though we were, progressing the barbecue idea seemed to be the next step.

Jon returned to the States and trusted us completely to get things underway. The first thing I had to do was to approach the churches in Canterbury. Everyone I spoke to thought the barbecue idea was a good one. The evangelical churches (six in Canterbury itself) really warmed to the idea; they could 'see it', as it were. The more traditional churches were at least content to bless the mission from a respectful distance.

I asked if I could do presentations to the congregations of the more positive churches and was given the opportunity to give a five-minute 'notice' on a Sunday morning. This I did – with remarkable results.

Now you, the reader, need to know that – in the UK

anyway, but also in many other countries – if you go into a church and ask for volunteers to take part in an evangelistic campaign, you will find people hiding under their seats, or at least avoiding your eyes. Basically, people are scared. It's not that they don't love the Lord, it's just that they don't know how to function in that context and would feel out of their depth trying. So it was with this in mind that I explained what we were going to do. There were four jobs (inviting, cooking, singing or hosting). I sketched out what each group would do. We needed volunteers. I then referred directly to people's aversion to evangelism. I told them that the previous year I had been asked to play the guitar on the St Luke's Church carnival float as part of the Maidstone Carnival. I had gone through the following thought process: people out there who *know me* will *see me*. With the kind of job I had, I felt this to be *inappropriate* and so said 'no'. And look at what I'm doing now! So (I continued), if on the one hand you feel that 'I don't do this kind of thing', and on the other hand you feel the Holy Spirit telling you, 'You will this time,' then I just want to say: I have no sympathy whatsoever!

I also let it be known that 50 people (the team we had put together earlier) from our church in Maidstone would be taking part. Surely they could match that!

Well, about 300 people signed up to take part – nothing short of a miracle. For some reason, people were excited about this initiative in *every* church – and wanted to take part. I remember in one church I had just completed explaining what we were going to do when a young lady came to the microphone and said, 'I had a dream last night in which I saw a dark storm cloud over Canterbury and it was about to pour with rain. I found it almost frightening and didn't know what it meant, but *this is it*! *This is it*!' The atmosphere was electric and there was a profound sense that God was in this. Loads of people signed up.

*   *   *

I now experienced (not for the last time) great favour from non-Christians towards what we were planning to do. I spoke to the council officials, who walked the streets with me and said things like, 'If you put one of your music groups here, you'll catch everyone on their way back to the bus station.' On another occasion, I stopped by Marks and Spencer in Canterbury, on the off chance that such an upmarket retailer might help out with the food in relation to the thousands of sausages and burgers we would need. I explained to the manager that I'd got myself into this unfortunate position of being the co-ordinator of the churches' outreach. Could they help? They readily agreed to do all the meat at half price. When I later tried to get the same deal in another town, the management were aghast that anyone could have offered such a discount! But so it was that, in the humorous skit at the end of the mission, I was able to say – in mock scriptural tones – that the organisers approached the Archangel Gabriel and asked, 'Wherein might we find 15,000 sausages?' The Archangel said, 'Try St Michael.' (Apologies to any non-British readers, who won't understand that one!)

But therein lay the rub. How many people were we to cook for? Since this had never been tried, there was no precedent on which to base our decision – and a wrong decision could result in a lot of hungry people, or a very large number of wasted sausages!

I had to make some sort of a calculation. This is the one I made: on an average day, we would apparently have about 130 team members. About 10 would be involved in the cooking side, and perhaps another 40 would be in worship bands. That would leave about 80, who would be able to approach passers-by and invite them to a free barbecue. They would each (I imagined) have a good contact every 10 minutes (seemed reasonable) and this would be on average with a group of two people. One in seven (say) of these groups or individuals would come. Well, *someone* had to calculate *something*! On the basis of this, we catered for 600 per day. Now, the basis of the calculation turned out to be totally wrong. In reality, we didn't talk to one person or group every ten minutes and it wasn't one in seven who came. And yet, the fact remains that the figure of 600 per day was *almost exactly right*. Indeed, in the years that have followed and in respect of the hundreds of thousands we have fed at free barbecues, the number of attendees has consistently averaged around 600 per day.

We had some churches and lots of team members. We had a plan. Now we needed money. Feeding 600 a day for two weeks was not, after all, going to be cheap.

I only ever made one phone call in respect of fundraising. This was to an eminent businessman, a knight of the realm who was chief executive of a £400 million company. Someone had suggested to me that he might be sympathetic and gave me a telephone number. I bit the bullet and phoned his office. Who, out of thousands of employees, should answer the phone when I asked for 'Sir Christopher'? I nearly fell off my chair when my interlocutor said simply, 'Speaking.'

I explained in halting terms about Americans, barbecues, street outreach and what-have-you and the result was that I heard the words, 'Well, from what you say, I do feel minded to support you. Come and see me at my home on Saturday and we'll talk more about it.'

So Saturday arrived and so did we – Gina and I, the four children, the dog. . . We were shown into this beautiful Elizabethan mansion and my host's opening gambit was to say, 'My wife and I have been praying about what you said and we do feel the Holy Sprit telling us to support you. What do you need?' I told him that we needed £5,000 to underpin the mission. 'A cheque will be with you in two days,' he said – and it was.

There was still a lot to do. We planned evening meetings, which needed a stage and lighting and a band to lead worship (the last of which was kindly supplied by friends from Holy Trinity Brompton in London, who commuted daily to Canterbury for six evening meetings). Then there was the invitation card to be designed and printed, a response card, badges for team members, a place for the team to meet in the mornings, rotas of musicians, borrowing barbecues, finding an electricity supply. This last item was donated by a local firm of solicitors for free, with a wire running from an upstairs window, across the path to a tree and then down – which gave rise to the line in our skit, 'And you shall receive power from on high. . .'

In fact, although there was loads to do, I had the one and only quiet six-week period in my job in my five years at the Kent Chamber. I was able to use office facilities (albeit paid for) and quite simply had the time to do all that needed to be done.

*　　*　　*

So the mission came, and with it the Americans. They were a motley bunch, good-hearted, some quite ordinary Christians, but also including no less than two Episcopalian bishops. Forty people in all, as promised.

Exactly a fortnight before the mission was due to start, *The Times* ran a front-page story stating that, commencing in two weeks, there would be the wettest two-week period since records began. So there we had it: the mission was set to begin in two weeks and last for two weeks. It was to be an entirely outdoor event.

The Saturday prior to the mission (starting Monday) was set aside as Training Day. Just how we were going to train people to do something we ourselves hadn't done remained to be seen. But Jon Shuler had been invited by Revd Kerry Thorpe, a vicar in nearby Margate, to hear Ed Silvoso, from Argentina, speak about the kind of evangelism they did there. Kerry had been one of the few to have received the vision for the mission from Jon as being from God and had promised to support it. This invitation now proved pivotal. Ed Silvoso spoke from Luke 10 about Jesus sending out the 72. And Jon, who had already felt God say that this chapter was to be central to the mission, heard Ed unpack a strategy and knew it to be God's strategy for our mission. The chapter records Jesus giving four particular instructions, in a certain order. The first is, 'Give them your peace.' The second, 'Eat what is set before you.' The third, 'Heal the sick who are there.' The fourth, 'Tell them the kingdom of God is near.'

So, basically, the first approach was to 'give our peace'. As Jesus said, 'If a man of peace is there, your peace will rest on him; if not, it will return to you' (v. 6). Through the worship, the generosity, the unjudgemental welcome afforded to all, we would do this and expect it to be received or rejected – but understanding that this peace was something quite tangible, which would evoke a response. Second, we would have fellowship with people – no strings attached. We would be on a level with them and make relationships. Third, we would seek to minister to their needs, through the laying on of hands if appropriate. But the question 'Could I pray for you?' (be it about the lost job, the broken relationships or the arthritis they had just been telling us about) would be a key. Finally, the declaration about the nearness of the kingdom would be a discussion of something that had first been demonstrated in deed rather than word.

Jon unpacked this to a crowded St Mary Bredin Church at the training day and I did most of the practical orientation. It was a wonderful day, with the Holy Spirit seeming to set out the agenda as we went along. Some felt that they wanted to prayer-walk the key sites on the Sunday evening and so we added that fixture at the last minute. About 60 people turned up. It has since become a regular part of what we do. We were discovering the formula as we went along.

On the Monday, the team turned up (praise God!). We met at 9.00 a.m. in the upper room of the church – an appropriate time of day and setting (see Acts 2) for the start of a move of the Spirit. After an hour of highly anointed worship (led by nothing more than a strummed guitar) and some organising into teams, we went out – apprehensive, but definitely ready to go. We had made no bones about the fact that the team members would feel like 'lambs among wolves' (Luke 10:3) and that was part of the package. But weakness could be turned to advantage. Wasn't it in our weakness that God's strength was made perfect? Best then, surely, to welcome weakness rather than try to eradicate it, and simply see what God would do.

We went out at 10.00 a.m. The weather was decent enough – something of a miracle, given the forecast in *The Times*. In the event, there was *not a drop of rain* on the barbecue mission for two weeks (and just five minutes of light rain at one of the evening meetings) and actually quite a lot of sunshine. Yet the very day after the mission ended, the rains started and there followed, as the newspapers later confirmed, the wettest two weeks since records began – starting exactly a fortnight late!

So we were on the streets, at last. As the worship bands started playing, there could be no doubt that the atmosphere started to change. This is what one team member wrote in his church magazine:

There was a real sense of God's presence and power at work in the whole of the city. There was a really refreshing feeling on the streets – there is something just so powerful about pure worship happening in the streets – everywhere you walked, all you could hear were the praises of God. God's Spirit was so evidently there; you felt you could reach out and touch it with your hands! . . . If you couldn't tell, being involved with the mission has really set me on fire for God!

It was true: as they resounded with worship, the streets did speak of God. The result was that many really did 'receive our peace' and respond positively to the invitation to come to Dane John Park, precisely because they loved the atmosphere of what was being offered – and frequently used the word 'peace' to describe it.

One of the most arresting features was the way in which the worship bands were put together each morning. 'Thrown together' would describe it more accurately. I would ask the guitarists to come forward. If there were eight or so, I would ask who was a 'strong' guitarist ('no false modesty, please') and put one in each of the four corners, accompanied by a not-so-strong guitarist. Then other musicians would come forward and a violinist would be sent to this corner, a flautist to that, a trumpeter to another; percussion people (tambourine, bongos, etc.) would be spread between the bands, and then singers (just ordinary Christians with a heart for worship) would be allocated, perhaps half a dozen to each band. Then they would be sent out, having had not so much as one minute collectively to practise anything. And yet, such was the freshness and genuineness of the worship – an explosion of pure joy on many occasions – that the worship was in fact highly attractive, as joy and enthusiasm always are. Furthermore, what the public was seeing was, quite obviously, *not* a bunch of musical experts (which would not have been an uncommon sight), but a bunch of ordinary people of all ages and all types who were having a ball. That *is* unusual.

People were also seeing 'the church' in a very public and high-profile way, in a completely new light. They were joyful, both young and old, numerous, united, generous, uncomplicated and *there* for people. So often we heard the remark, 'This is the kind of thing the churches ought to be doing.'

*   *   *

From midday people were able to come to the barbecue itself, which was set to last until 2.00 p.m. each day (precisely the timing we have used since then). All the food being prepared, all the other kinds of preparation work, all the prayer and anticipation. . . Would anyone actually turn up to this barbecue?

Come midday, there was *a queue for the food* – a queue which stayed pretty consistent for two hours a day, six days a week for two weeks. In fact, we fed nearly 8,000 people during that mission and – most strikingly – 90 per cent of them were people who would never have darkened the doors of a church.

Something was going on here! It wasn't just that the Christians were being mobilised to an unusual extent; nor simply that hundreds of non-Christians were turning up (quite unusual for evangelistic meetings in the UK today); it was also that the presence of God was so manifest – so obvious – that even non-Christians were talking about it. Guests would regularly open up about their most intimate secrets to complete strangers on the team, allowing themselves to be prayed for; and they were quite naturally talking about Jesus, even without anyone trying too hard to bring the conversation round to that subject. It just happened.

Every day that we did the barbecue, a number would

willingly give their lives to Christ for the first time; others would give their names and addresses. Still more were obviously touched by Christ, obviously moved, sometimes in tears, and would frequently return the next day for more. We were starting to get a following of people who knew us and began to trust us. This was particularly so of the homeless, who sat without problem alongside housewives, businesspeople, college students and tourists.

Many team members' lives were also changed through the mission. Not least Gina's – and the homeless had a lot to do with it.

She had gone through a difficult period in the two years since my 'calling' in that, even though she was fully supportive of what was happening (the Lord had, after all, asked for her 'permission' to call me), she had begun to count the cost in her thoughts. For two years, conscious that my salary would presumably plummet in the not-too-distant future, she started (for the first time ever) to notice the expensive jewellery that Chamber members' wives typically wore to the functions we organised, and to grieve for the fact that we would have to give up many aspects of the well-to-do life we were leading. But at Canterbury she started to befriend a number of homeless people. On one occasion she spoke to a man whose partner had just died, whom he had 'loved to bits'; he was addicted to heroin and pretty much everything else going; and he couldn't stand to live indoors, so 'locked' had he become within the homeless way of life. Gina felt that she touched his desolation. Here was a man who had absolutely nothing – no life and no hope. And at that moment Gina realised how rich she was in terms of the things that really mattered.

That man was led to Christ. His wider bequest on that occasion was to leave Gina a changed person and she never again worried (much!) about jewellery or the other fancies of life.

Other team members became changed by the experience of being used by God, finding that the Lord could speak through them, and that they could flow in a move of the Spirit that was all around them, and that any test of how 'good' they were at evangelism turned out to be totally irrelevant. It was a question of doing what we saw the Father doing and just fitting in with it – and he was doing a lot.

By the time the final celebration came on Monday the 9th June, the church – packed with about 250 team members – had an electric atmosphere. Jon asked team members to come forward to the microphone and say what the last two weeks had meant to them, and they did, without ceasing, for two and a half hours. One after the other came to say that what we had experienced had been special, unique in their experience; that God had 'set before us an open door that none could close'; and that we must continue to go through it. There was a tremendous and general sense of *significance* about what had happened.

It could surely not stop here.

Part 2

4

Moving Out

If something of significance had happened, it wasn't immediately obvious whether or how it would have any direct impact on my personal future. I still had a calling that I didn't know how to fulfil. Nothing had altered. At the end of the mission I knew I had to turn up for work at the Kent Chamber of Commerce once again, and I was not aware of any likely change to that.

On Sunday the 8th June, however, the day after the last barbecue in Canterbury and the day before the final celebration, something further happened to shake the foundations of our normal life. To be specific, I resigned my job (more or less) – without meaning to.

It just happened, like this: I had a phone call on the Sunday from the chief executive of Kent TEC (an organisation with which the Chamber was discussing a merger). He had never phoned me on a Sunday before and he never did again. It wasn't even that important – just something about a meeting the following day. But he did hit this remarkable moment in my life, the climax of the Canterbury mission. And I said (or more accurately, I found myself saying) that if the merger went ahead, I would not be wanting a position in the new company, but would be leaving. He was very surprised. So was I! Until now, the discussion had been about what position I would hold. But there it was. I had just said something of the greatest importance.

I put the phone down and Gina said, 'What have you said?'

'I don't know,' I replied. 'It just came out!'

Now started a remarkable two-week period in the run-up to the Chamber's monthly board meeting, where I would give my formal resignation if I went ahead with the idea. But was this what I was supposed to do? This one I had to get right. And yet, I had a profound sense that *now was the time*. 'Now you walk on the water' was the phrase ringing in my ears. But how would I earn a living? Was this really the Lord impelling me to leave – with nothing to go to? Scary.

We decided to lay out a fleece. Kent TEC was much the larger organisation and their chief executive was to get the top job, with five other bodies merging together into a new body. I had been holding out for the deputy chief executive post in the merged body. The problem had been that there was no plan for such a post. But the final management structure was to be decided within days (itself an amazing coincidence of God's timing). We agreed that, if I were offered the deputy chief executive position, I would accept it. If not, I would leave – for work itself would be *driving* me out, even while God was calling me out. That would be conclusive.

The management structure was duly decided. I was to be director of membership and marketing. After nearly two years of discussion, it got to this point at exactly the moment when I needed to know what I was to be offered. Days later, the board meeting got under way and the proposed management structure was duly accepted. I urged them to accept it, saying that I didn't think we could achieve better in the circumstances. (They too had wanted me to be deputy chief executive, not least to boost the Chamber's standing in the merged company.) I then told them (having warned the chairman of my intentions) that I would be leaving. I would support the merger and give it till the end of the year to pilot the Chamber safely into the merged company; then I would leave.

I can only say that I was acting under a strong inner compulsion in doing this. But that didn't make it any easier to do, as I knew I was disappointing many people, even hurting them, not least because many in the Chamber had relied on me to fight its corner within the new merged organisation. The worst was when I had to tell my staff, the 17 or so in the central office of the Chamber, that I would be leaving. This was minutes after the end of the board meeting, and it was a heavy moment. There were tears amongst the staff and I felt totally wretched about what I was doing.

After this most moving meeting, I retreated into my office for some privacy and consolation. I needed both! Then the phone rang. It was Sir Christopher Wates, the person who had helped us out financially with the Canterbury mission a few weeks before. 'Guess what I've just done,' I said. I told him I had just given up my job. He seemed quite relaxed about the idea and said, 'I tell you what we should do: why don't you and Gina come round to dinner one

Saturday night and we'll talk about what we can do to get things moving along the lines that we saw in Canterbury, but more widely across Kent and Sussex.'

That was it! That was what I was going to do. The penny dropped there and then, and I thank God for Chris Wates' intervention at that very moment, minutes after I had resigned. But it seems that I had to take the leap of faith *first*, without knowing the destination, before the Lord revealed what was next.

In retrospect, it looks so obvious, that this was what I was going to do – to take the barbecue idea, in the context of this wonderful move of the Spirit, and seek to apply it more widely. But it hadn't even been a thought until Chris Wates made the suggestion; and the suggestion wasn't made until I had taken the step of resigning my job.

*   *   *

The dinner was arranged and, beforehand, we got thinking. Various parts of my work background were able to kick in at this point. I had been involved in membership organisations from the start, where the key was to generate involvement and activity 'at the grass roots'. I had worked for the Jubilee Centre, which ran the Keep Sunday Special Campaign and in 1986 won a remarkable reprieve for the Christian Sunday by organising public meetings in 200 constituencies, mostly on the same night – 14th February, 'Operation Valentine'. I had subsequently been with the British Chambers of Commerce (the Chambers' national HQ), which had been about galvanising 100 local Chambers into action, and their 100,000 businesses in membership. In

the Conservative Party, it was 650 constituency organisations and half a million members. In the Kent Chamber, it
was the ten local Chambers and our 4,000 member compa-
nies and their senior managers. How, then, was I now to
involve churches and team members in something that
would be, not a flash in the pan, but something ongoing?

We started formulating plans about how an organisation
we started might seek to have a programme of missions,
with team members from one town coming to help in
another. We could offer a service to groups of churches,
offering presentations in churches to recruit the team, providing training for the team, plus equipment, badges, invitation cards, public liability insurance, etc., making life
much easier for busy pastors – and avoiding the constant
reinvention of the wheel. Team members could be expected
to support the project with donations (they certainly had in
Canterbury), and a 'movement' could begin. Piloting this
locally in Kent and Sussex made sense too. After a period,
it could then go national.

We needed a name. Gina prayed and said it should be
'something to do with moving or movement'. I said, 'On the
Move.'

We should form a charitable trust, and for that we
needed trustees. We asked Kerry Thorpe, a church leader
involved from the beginning, and Edwin Boorman, a senior
businessman in Kent and a lovely Christian. And then it
was time to go to dinner with the Wateses.

As part of a wonderful evening of sharing and strategis-
ing, Chris and Georgie read the draft leaflet I had come up
with. They felt the whole thing was truly exciting. They
knew the Lord had moved in Canterbury. Their hearts were

fully engaged. We asked Chris to become the third trustee and our first chairman. He said he'd think about it. He and I met again in London and he questioned me closely. Then he said 'yes'. We had a board.

I went to see a couple of local bishops in Kent and Sussex. Both were most affirmative. Through my Chamber contacts, British Gas Transco gave us computers, Barclays Bank desks. The Chamber's Christmas luncheon arrived, along with 300 local businesspeople, and others had organised for glowing tributes to be made. I went out on a high.

I also went out with a 'package'. This seemed just as well, as my prayer that we would raise £30,000 for On the Move before it started was spectacularly *not* answered. We managed to raise just £700, which doesn't last a family of six long, never mind the expenses of setting up a new organisation.

Our first fixture was to go to the USA for two weeks in January 1998 (the 1st January marking the start of our new life), to help Jon Shuler do a barbecue mission *à la* Canterbury there. Only, when we – and the team of nine others who came with us – got there, we found that it wasn't set to be as *à la* Canterbury as we'd thought. Jon's wife showed us where bands were to play and where the inviting was to take place. Gina and I both asked, 'But where are the people?' It was all but empty, being low season on Myrtle Beach (a busy place at other times of the year). It then turned out that the place we were to invite people *to* was 20 minutes' drive from the inviting point. There was more.

The meal was very kindly being provided at a knock-down price by a Christian disaster relief organisation – but was not really the right food for this kind of event. And the meal itself was really not 'the main event', as before. The key task was to 'hold' people at the meal (in a sort of side marquee), so that they wouldn't go before 'the main event' started, which was a presentation of music, drama and preaching in the big top, which held 400 people. The big top, being low season, had been given for free. But this was surely missing the point. Our hearts sank.

The problem was that this mission was driven by a young man who had come to Canterbury with Jon, and dear Jon himself had been pressed into service as chairman of something that wasn't really his idea. When we told Jon that we couldn't see it working, his face fell (a sort of 'yeah, I know, but I don't want to face it' look). He must have figured that, because the die had been cast, he should put a brave face on it – and he did so better than I could have done.

The mission started with about 70 team members and ended with about 25 (11 of them English), as disappointing numbers and a four-fifths-empty big top sapped morale. Actually, God still moved and a number of people came to faith in spite of the circumstances. But it was a humiliating experience for Jon, and a steep learning curve for all of us. Clearly, the human dynamics of people flows, distances to be travelled and what would actually work were vitally important, and could not be brushed aside in an 'act of faith'.

The mission ended. On the final Sunday of our trip we went to church, a big Episcopalian church where the Holy Spirit was free to move. We sat in the gallery – and for some reason I found I couldn't stop weeping. I just wept and wept. I was thinking about what we were going home to, and what I'd done in giving up my job. How was I to feed my family? It was all too much. People were called forward for ministry at the end, and I went. Taken to a prayer room at the back, I cried uncontrollably for another half an hour until it all subsided and I felt better. But back home, I would still have to face the music.

*   *   *

And some music it turned out to be! The first shock centred on my leaving package. What I had managed to negotiate was the payment of a year's salary and benefits to compensate me for my loss of office (as I was truly not offered an 'equivalent position'). It was agreed between the TEC and the Chamber that £61,000 would be paid to me, and that the TEC would be the paymaster. I never actually got anything in writing, because right up to Christmas Eve there was continued to-ing and fro-ing about the exact text of a letter the TEC was to send the Chamber to seal the agreement, and in the end I had to leave on trust or else change my mind on the whole thing. But I did trust the word of senior businesspeople and didn't think too much of it – until we returned from the USA, that is, and started to hear that the TEC wasn't going to pay up.

The TEC had always been at best ambivalent towards both me and the Chamber (the implicit competition between these business-support bodies being part of the logic of the merger). Now they started demanding assurances from the Chamber that it could 'afford to pay' my redundancy package (even though the deal was that it wouldn't have to, because it couldn't!), as a precondition for the TEC to pay the money. Absurd!

At any rate, Gina and I were left high and dry. A year's salary had been a very good basis on which to launch out into something new. As it was, there was now turning out to be nothing. My statutory entitlement of three months salary was still payable by the Chamber (about £17,000, before tax), but since it didn't really have that kind of money available, it wasn't at all clear whether I'd see any of that, and if so when. So we had literally nothing.

What was I to do about the TEC's refusal to pay? What did God want me to do? Turn the other cheek? Seek justice? Either approach could be validated by Scripture and so I needed to know what the Lord was saying to us, now. I had no written record of the agreement, which would be a problem in taking the matter to court. On the other hand, there was plenty of goodwill from the Chamber chairman and others, who thought I was being shabbily treated.

It was the 2nd February 1998 when it became quite clear that the TEC wasn't paying up. Crucially, I asked for guidance in a very specific form. Every day, there's a Scripture verse in *The Times*, just by the 'Births, Marriages and Deaths' column. I asked the Lord, 'Please guide me through the Scripture verse in today's *Times*.'

I looked it up. This is what it said: 'I, the LORD, will appear before you in court, quick to testify against sorcerers, adulterers and perjurers, against those who cheat the hired labourer of his wages. . .' (Malachi 3:5)

Wow! WOW!! WOW!!! Was that clear, or what?

So we decided. . . to take the TEC to court.

In fact, it would be an industrial tribunal in the first

instance. The applications went in and we waited to see what would come of it.

*   *   *

Meanwhile, things were not going too well on the evangelism front. We had started On the Move (OTM). The trustees had met and a bank account had been opened. But there was not, alas, anything much to put in it. Money came in incredibly slowly. Always there were hopeful signs and I was ever the optimist. This or that meeting coming up, or the application to this or that trust, would produce something. I was asked to preach at the City Church in Canterbury, the one where the young woman had had the dream about rain clouds over Canterbury just ahead of the previous summer's mission. This I did and, shortly afterwards, they sent OTM a cheque for £500 – the only significant donation in our first few months. (Little did they know how significant that donation was.) Otherwise, it was a lean time on both the work and home fronts. On the Move had no money to pay us a salary, and therefore didn't. Meanwhile, the Chamber couldn't pay me my notice either. To make matters worse, an idea for a second Canterbury mission in June 1998 was moving forward at an agonisingly slow pace, as two of the key leaders couldn't agree on the dates. It looked as though it might not happen at all.

Added to this, our first mission, in Rochester at the beginning of April (a spin-off from a Springboard mission that Michael Green was leading – and it was he who wanted an On the Move component), couldn't even pay its way. One church put up about a third of the money needed to pay for the food, another one added a bit more, but two or three other churches taking part were not able to contribute anything. So we had to pay for more than half of the direct costs of the Rochester mission from our own meagre resources. Yet we were willing to do so, so keen were we to demonstrate at the earliest opportunity that this really worked.

Praise God – it did work. In fact, the headline on our first ever newsletter was 'It Worked – Alleluia!' It was a smallish mission and we had only about 70 team members, working for two days in a very suitable location, with a patch of grass owned by the cathedral right on the side of the high street being made available for the barbecue.

There were several things that were particularly encouraging about Rochester. The Holy Spirit showed up, for one thing. That was actually important for me to see and confirm. After all, the Canterbury mission had been founded on Jon Shuler's vision and was a very special 'one-off'. And yet here was that wonderful anointing on the streets again. We also had the favour of the people again. (Indeed, a local pub owner I spoke to in the run-up asked me out of the blue if I wanted to borrow his white plastic tables and chairs for the mission. At Canterbury people sat on the grass, but this was much better and we never looked back in this respect.) We saw miracles with the weather again. On the first day, it rained during the morning and at 11.55 – five minutes before the barbecue was due to start – it stopped raining and the sun came out. We borrowed J-cloths from a local greengrocers, quickly dried the tables and chairs and, on the dot of 12.00, the barbecue was open for business and there was the customary queue for food. It ended at 2.00 p.m. At 2.05 the heavens opened.

The main thing was that the heavens had opened in the more important sense during the intervening two hours. We were able to see the team inspired, once again. One extra encouragement concerned Michael Green. He was there with us on the first day (having made space from his various mission engagements to 'come and see'). What he saw, he absolutely loved. He was thrilled to see so many non-Christians there. He was thrilled with the atmosphere – so non-threatening and 'cringe free', as he later described it. And he was astounded by the eight people who, seemingly out of nowhere, made first-time Christian commitments that lunchtime.

So Michael privately resolved to do something about it and promote this new form of evangelism. He wrote a full-page article for the *Church of England Newspaper*, headed 'Cringe Free Evangelist Takes to the Streets'. His piece ended up: 'Give it a try. It is imaginative, it is effective and it is great fun!'

He also approached the *Church Times*, who duly sent a reporter and photographer to the Maidstone mission that July, with a two-page spread and eight colour photos devoted to On the Move in the next issue. That year we also did a mission in Brixham in Devon, and the Baptist church there took it upon themselves to write to the *Baptist Times* about what they had seen – and the *Baptist Times* subsequently did a big spread. It was the same with the United Reformed Church in Tonbridge, with a URC publication. The result was that we started getting enquiries from further afield.

At the same time, immediately after the Rochester mission was over, a significant number of team members started making monthly donations to OTM by banker's order. And then, joy of joys, one of my applications for funding, this time to the Jerusalem Trust, came good. (Another Michael Green intervention had been significant here.) The trust gave us £10,000 and a promise of more over the next two years. Someone else, who had not wanted to 'carry the can' alone, immediately responded to the Jerusalem Trust grant by making a similarly sized donation. Suddenly, we were airborne! Gina and I were paid a salary at the end of April for the first time, and our back-pay too. This was just as well, since by then we had gone for three months without income and were about three weeks away from having to sell our house, just to live. It was a very happy ending to a very difficult period.

*   *   *

Around this time I had a meeting with the Chamber chairman, who came bearing good tidings. Apparently, Kent TEC didn't want the bad publicity of a tribunal hearing and they might be prepared to settle for £30,000, in addition to the £17,000 which was just starting to come from the Chamber. Would I agree to that? I said that I would. A couple of weeks later the deal was done, in a telephone conversation between a solicitor friend of mine, who had been acting for us, and the TEC's solicitor, just two days before the tribunal hearing. The tribunal was cancelled.

By now we had lined up a total of five missions for our first year. The strapline of our first leaflet, 'A thousand Christians moving together in evangelism', was starting to look realistic, incredulous though some had been back in

December on first seeing the draft leaflet. We bought our own equipment – 20 white plastic tables and 100 chairs, plus a whizzo commercial barbecue griddle, which (we later found out) was capable of cooking for well over 1,000 people per lunchtime.

When I went to a biggish charismatic church in Ashford one Sunday to present the vision of OTM and to see who might like to sign up to become team members, the pastor took me aside. They were going, he said, to ask the congregation to respond to something else at the end of the service. He didn't want to confuse matters by mixing the response to one call with the response to another. So would I please do my bit in the middle of the service and ask people who wanted to sign up to do so there and then? That seemed to be OK (I didn't want the mix-up either). So I said I'd give it a go. I did my five-minute presentation about what we did and how people could help, and then said something like, 'Well, you've had plenty of time to think about it! Who wants to take part? Go on . . . put your hands up!' And with this, loads of people, amused at the boldness of the proposition, put their hands up and were willing to fill in the form then and there.

Someone later said to me that this was a perfectly biblical approach. After all, when Jesus went up to people and said 'Follow me', it tends to say that 'immediately' they followed him. When the Holy Spirit gives vision, it is so often an immediate thing and the passage of time only serves to give Satan the opportunity to sow doubt ('I'll think about it . . . I'm not sure if I can spare the time . . . I'll decide later'), often leading to no decision at all. The Holy Spirit really is giving vision at the time of the presentation. The thing is to 'catch the moment'. It's not manipulation; it's envisioning. If people later find that they can't (or don't want to) take part, they can easily opt out.

This single unplanned innovation produced a revolution in my productivity. First, the response in the service was at least twice as high as it had normally been when I said, 'Come and see me after the service.' Second, the 'after the service' approach meant that I could normally do just one presentation on a Sunday morning. So presenting to six churches in a town would take six Sundays. The number of missions that could be attempted in any one summer was strictly limited by this. But if it was a case of a five-minute presentation followed by a five-minute sign-up time and then out, how many presentations could be attempted on a single Sunday morning?

So it was that, when we went to do the recruiting for the Tonbridge mission, a driver was provided, a route was worked out locally, and a schedule was created for me to do presentations at six churches on the same Sunday morning. It was actually quite theatrical as I arrived in a new church halfway through their service, yet expected. The person leading the service would say, as I arrived at the back of the church, 'Ah, there he is now. . .' and I would be brought to the front to do my five minutes. At the end of two Sundays in Tonbridge, I had done twelve presentations and come away with over 200 team members signed up to take part.

5

A Higher Gear

So there we were, fresh faced and bushy tailed, and with lots of hope . . . and almost no experience. But June proved to be a pivotal month in two respects. First, although the deal had been done with Kent TEC about my redundancy payment, they inexplicably now changed their minds, yet again. We found this out when I investigated why we hadn't yet received a cheque. The new Chamber chief executive was equally surprised to hear that we hadn't had one, as was the chairman. We contacted our solicitor friend who had clinched the deal for us in a telephone conversation with his opposite number. When he now tried to phone her, she appeared to avoid him and didn't return calls. Finally he managed to speak to her, and she denied that any deal had been done.

Our solicitor friend, Jonathan Coad (one-time member of our Christian rock band in my Cambridge days, and my best man at our wedding), said that he would act for us for free. This was quite something as he was now a top London solicitor, with clients ranging from Nigel Mansell to David Beckham and the Duchess of York. He did, however, warn us that – were we to lose – we could end up with a big legal bill, as we would be liable for the TEC's legal expenses. We had nothing in writing and, although Jonathan himself had concluded the deal, it could be difficult to prove. But the Lord's leading through *The Times* Scripture verse had been so clear that it seemed inevitable we should decide to press on and start county court proceedings. As we were soon to realise, however, we would have to be represented in court by a barrister and Jonathan couldn't provide *that* service for us for free. This, we were advised, would cost about £5,000. Where could we find that kind of money? The whole point was that we were owed money and consequently didn't have it, and therefore couldn't afford the process of getting it! Not only did we realise this, we were quite sure that the TEC was relying on it. In their view, we surmised, it would never come to court. They only had to wait for us to give up on financial grounds.

We were actually (and somewhat disobediently) wondering whether to do just that when someone (or the Lord, through someone) stepped in. It was the chairman of the local newspaper, the *Kent Messenger* Group. He phoned me up, and explained that he and the newspaper were highly concerned about how I had been treated and had resolved to do something about it. He, the chairman, had spoken to the editorial board – unasked by me – and they had agreed to release £5,000 (it just so happened) to help us fight the case. With Jonathan's continued help, and this budget at our disposal, we had everything we needed. I don't know how often newspapers offer people money, with no strings attached, to seek justice, but that is what happened here. The TEC, who knew nothing of the help we were receiving from these two quarters, must have been mystified to hear that we were continuing with the action, a David-and-Goliath-type contest though it remained.

The second key development in June 1998 was a dose of envisioning from the Lord, which appeared to be out of all proportion to who we were and the stage we had reached. Sometimes God kick-starts a process, suddenly giving it vastly added momentum. Sometimes he gives a 'stretched' vision, which seems too large for the person or people to whom he is giving it. Both happened here, *par excellence*. Bear in mind that we had been going for less than six months and had done precisely one mission.

This is how God moved things along. I was sitting in my church one Sunday evening – another occasion when I was not really listening to what was going on, but was lost in thought. (I really do normally listen in church – honest!) Something came upon me, in the form of a heavy weight pressing down on my shoulders – pressing hard and continuously for several minutes. It was a powerful and intense experience, the like of which I had never known. It was as if I was wearing a coat of heavy chain mail and it was pressing down, pressing down, pressing down. I knew God wanted to speak to me. Clear as a bell, I heard these words: 'Your vision for the millennium year is not big enough.' I don't think it was what people call 'an audible voice'. It was an inner voice, but I heard it once only (once was enough), and it carried unmistakeable authority.

After a few minutes, the weight lifted and I was left pondering what had happened.

Life is frequently busy and I was taken over by busyness for the next 24 hours, having no time to reflect on this profound experience – until the next evening. The moment I had time, I walked around our garden for what turned out to be three hours, asking, 'What do you mean, Lord? What do you mean?' I started to see things with greater and greater clarity and to draw some key conclusions.

The first thing that came to me was that this form of mission could work in cities. These were the hardest places for the gospel, but the free barbecues were suited to cities as well as towns, not least because each city in England is really a collection of towns – or big villages. Second, one could have a city mission, which was actually a collection of more local 'town' missions all happening at once. For example, in London the mission could potentially take place with one group of churches in Camden Town, while another group was doing the same thing in King's Cross, another in Islington, and so on. All in all, what I was realising that evening was that the Lord wanted us to do missions in the ten biggest cities of England in the year 2000, with multi-site missions in each.

Now, that was a big vision! It would require thousands of team members, hundreds of worship bands, large amounts of equipment (chairs and tables, barbecues), transport, staff, office equipment, literature – and most crucially the support of the church, all denominations working together, in each of these cities. And this was to be taken forward by an unknown and untried husband-and-wife team, who had so far done precisely one mission – and who had no significant resources of any kind.

I discussed all this with Gina, and she felt it was from the Lord. The next morning, over breakfast, I shared it with an American friend who was staying with us – a veteran of the

Canterbury mission. I asked her what she thought. She turned to Gina and said, 'What do *you* think?' Gina replied simply that she thought it was wonderful, but was looking at it from a practical point of view. For example, we would need a second car. Now Anne, our friend, looked meaningfully at Gina and said, 'Gina, the way you will know that these ideas are from God is when someone offers you a second car.' An interesting idea, but we thought nothing more of it until that evening, when a friend phoned to say that he and his wife had been in the supermarket that morning and had both independently heard God say to them that they should *give us their spare car*. He was phoning up to ask if we wanted a second car. . .

These sorts of things hit you in a peculiar way. The Americans call such things 'awesome' (they call pretty much everything awesome!), and 'awe' is perhaps the best way to describe what we felt. It was as if we were standing on holy ground. God had spoken. He was now confirming his word most clearly through other people.

I have to admit that this was a great sign. But it wasn't such a good car!

*   *   *

How to proceed on this? We were just into our second and third missions, both tremendously fruitful. But shortly afterwards, we had the space to think. One conclusion we came to was that we should arrange to have the next mission filmed. We needed a video as a tool to give an insight to church leaders up and down the country into what we were proposing – something that would demonstrate the heart of On the Move as well as show what we actually did and how we did it. The next mission would be Tonbridge. We arranged for the mission to be filmed on Saturday the 1st August 1998. A one-day take was all we could afford. 'Lord, please make it a good day!'

It started out an awful day. The Tonbridge mission had proved to be the most difficult mission we had encountered – not because the churches were un-keen, or the team was in any way inadequate, nor because of some kind of problem with the weather. It was the *spiritual* climate we were up against. From the first day of the mission, we had encountered something we hadn't yet seen much of – opposition. It was as if the people of the town didn't *like* us (the churches, that is). One charming individual put loud-speakers pointing out of his upstairs window, blaring out obscene heavy metal music just above where a worship band was sited. Several people were gratuitously rude when offered an invitation to a free barbecue. One man said he could never forgive the church because he had once been refused permission to lean his bicycle against a church building. Youths started cycling through the audience at an evening meeting we had in the grounds of Tonbridge Castle, just to antagonise us. What was going on? What could we do about it? We struggled on, not knowing the answer.

Gina and I were at a loss. It wasn't exactly a bad mission. One or two came to faith. But there was not the freedom we had experienced elsewhere and it all seemed like hard work. Of course, we prayed. And we prayed and we prayed! But there was no breakthrough. And so it was that we drove towards Tonbridge on the morning of Saturday the 1st August (the day the video crew was coming) in the slough of depression, feeling that we had nothing left to give and having no clue as to how we could see the Lord's victory here.

Then something highly unusual happened. Gina often gave messages in tongues in our private prayer times. But now we were at the morning meeting at our church team base, with 150 team members praising God, and Gina turned to me and said, 'I have a message in tongues.' It was risky, in that one didn't know what many team members would make of such a thing. But I said, 'Go for it,' and Gina, brave as always, said to the team members that she had a tongue and proceeded to give it. Now the atmosphere turned electric. There was a pregnancy in the Spirit. The interpretation came, not from me, but from about 15 different team members, each of whom added a bit in a marvellous piece of 'body ministry', revealing bit by bit what God was saying. What he was saying was this: 'You need to listen to Tonbridge; Tonbridge is hurting; Tonbridge has been hurt by the church.'

Then we discussed it. Someone, a local, said that he had heard the story that hundreds of years ago the church authorities in Tonbridge had actually stolen the poor fund and spent it on themselves. Others concurred. Another told the story of what had apparently happened in the mid-nineteenth century when the railway workers arrived in what was to become a railway hub. They came to the parish church and said they would like to worship there. The members of the parish church met together and said, 'If their kind come, we're leaving.' The railway workers were informed that they were not welcome. And so on. The scars of the history of Tonbridge started to be revealed. They were scars the people bore as a result of the direct actions of the church. What became clear was that the contemporary generation of Tonbridge residents had, as it were, 'received' a dislike for the church, without knowing why they should have such an attitude. It was in the DNA of Tonbridge, if you like, that the church was disliked, from generation to generation – a 'spiritual stronghold' if ever I saw one.

The church leaders present felt that this 'steer' really was from God and that the first response should be one of repentance. They therefore led us in a moving time of saying 'sorry' to God, on behalf of the church in Tonbridge over the generations, for these past sins, which had produced such bitter fruit. There was a very genuine spirit of repentance in the room and, finally, we all felt that we had done what was required of us – and went out onto the streets.

I want to digress for a moment, before I finish the story of the Tonbridge mission. I had been introduced to repentance of this kind just ten weeks before, in Dallas, Texas, of all places. I had been invited there by Roger Mitchell, one of the main speakers at an international conference there, and, as he had paid for my airfare, I felt I couldn't refuse when he asked me to be one of seven Englishmen to come onstage at a certain point in his talk, and together publicly repent for the historic hurts that England had caused America. I went onstage at the appointed moment, before 8,000 Americans, without really feeling any personal conviction about what we were doing. In fact, I found it a bit embarrassing to be one of seven Englishmen to lie down on the stage in an act of public contrition. What I never expected was that, as I did so, the Holy Spirit would take over and I would find myself in floods of tears, deeply moved in my heart and taking part in a very genuine expression of grief. What was going on here? I had to find out! It was clear that many in the audience were profoundly touched, and then representatives from the American church repented in turn for their sins towards the British – and something happened there too, bringing a release in the Spirit that was too obvious to discount.

Part of the explanation came to me when, on our return journey, we were messed about by the airline and lost 24 hours as a result – totally its fault. It was when one of its representatives came to us and apologised, profusely and genuinely, on behalf of the airline, that we all felt better, and better able to forgive and let go of our anger and frustration. Now, the key point for me was this: the person who apologised was just a representative, and we all knew that it was not *his* fault. Yet, even though he was not personally responsible, his apology carried weight because it was made *on behalf of the corporation he represented*. In that case, it started to make a bit more sense that Roger and his seven Englishmen could apologise for the sins of English people 200 years before (not our fault) and yet carry weight with Americans now.

What seemed to be going on was that people carry hurts and resentments down the generations, as it were, and even inherited anger and resentment can be a block to the Holy Spirit, just as personal anger and resentment are. Forgiveness of others is a key to receiving God's blessing. When someone who has hurt you apologises, it helps you to forgive. So apologising to 8,000 Americans helped them to be able to release forgiveness in respect of deeply felt (but little recognised) hurts and resentments. As one releases forgiveness, the Holy Spirit moves in. Makes sense, doesn't it?

In the days that followed the Dallas experience, I remember saying to Roger that one of the things that needed to be apologised for was the church's attitude to non-Christians. How many times over the generations had we in the church hurt people outside the church by our judgemental attitude, our 'holier than thou' hypocrisy, and our implication that others were not good enough to join us until they changed (as we supposedly had)? How different from Jesus' saying that it is only the sick that have need of a physician.

Back to Tonbridge. As you will understand, I was in some way prepared for what was going on there. What I didn't expect (but should have) was that the Lord would ask me to apologise for the sins of the church in Tonbridge, publicly, at the barbecue. It was only when the barbecue was in full swing, with about 300 members of the public there (we fed 900 that day), that I felt the Lord say, 'Now you go to the microphone and apologise on behalf of the church.' I knew I had the authority to do so, because the church leaders had so embraced what the Lord seemed to be saying. So I had to go for it.

I went to the microphone and said, quite simply, that we had been praying and that God had shown us that the church had hurt the people of Tonbridge (I told the story of the railway workers) and that in response to this, we really wanted to say how sorry we were – if they felt able to receive this apology. I was also able to say that, in hurting people in this way, we had misrepresented the image of God and the truth was that, unlike the 'no' they had received from the church, there was a 'yes' for them from God.

That was all I said. Yet the atmosphere changed instantly. People were suddenly ready to receive us – and our message. Many came to the Lord that day (including three teenage lads who had cycled through the audience to antagonise us at the previous evening's meeting). It finished as a great mission, with an unmistakeable sense of breakthrough.

It also happened that this was the day of mission captured on video. The particular message of apology was also filmed, and became the centrepiece of the video we produced to bring the vision of On the Move to the ten cities for the millennium year. Church leaders up and down the country were moved by the apology, and the sense that we were trying to put something right by 'coming out' was beautifully received. It became part of the ethos of On the Move thereafter.

*   *   *

By September, the video editing process was complete and the first person we played it to loved it so much that he phoned up Roger Mitchell (of Dallas fame) there and then, saying that Roger must play the video at his conference of city networkers the following week. Roger invited us to come, and the contacts with Leeds in particular were made that way. Other contacts were made through a seminar I was invited to do at New Wine.

Now we were in launch mode for the 'Missions 2000' vision, and there started a process of finding out who in each city brought church leaders together and then calling them (usually cold-calling them) to explain the vision.

Now, it's a pretty naff thing to do to phone a senior leader and explain that one believes God has given one a vision to do a mission in their city. But this I did and they were not only gracious, but frequently enthusiastic. The barbecue concept was an easy verbal picture to paint, and people tended to 'get it' immediately. I think two of them said something to the effect that, 'We've been looking for something to do together for the millennium year and I believe this is it!'

So doors were starting to open dramatically. It wasn't an altogether straightforward process, however. For example, the person I first spoke to wasn't always the person who would take it forward. Indeed, it got stuck with the 'wrong person' for months on a couple of occasions before we sought out somebody else and then saw release. Another problem was trying to do it from Kent. A visit to Teesside, for example, involved a 5.30 a.m. departure and a late-night return, with only about two or three hours up there to do any useful work. And work there was, once a presentation had been made, because different potential venues within each city had to be explored, local groupings of churches addressed, and then contacts pursued in order to form each mission. All this times ten!

There were many visits; many presentations; much travelling. The vision was received wonderfully – for example by about 50 pastors from Birmingham who invited us to their retreat conference, or by 50 pastors from Manchester at their monthly meeting, or by 20 or so leaders of a Luis Palau mission committee in Sheffield. Without exception, the city-wide presentations were ethusiastically received. Each time there was an atmosphere of inspiration and excitement – and unreserved welcome. Dates were made over the next twelve months for missions in all ten cities and we subsequently worked hard to develop the content of each mission.

One of the most remarkable happenings concerned Spring Harvest, the Easter-time gathering of tens of thousands of evangelical Christians, an annual event that is a key part of the UK Christian calendar and, I gather, the largest event of its kind in Europe. It was shortly after I had the vision about the ten cities that in a time of prayer I clearly 'saw' myself speaking to thousands from the main stage at Spring Harvest and telling them what was to happen in the big cities during 2000. It was to be not so much an advertisement as a wake-up call for the church, with God telling his church that it was time to 'arise, shine, for your light has come' (Isaiah 60:1). The thing I saw most clearly was me asking the audience to stand and then welcoming onstage a lone trumpeter, who proceeded to play a trumpet call – representing the 'wake-up call' for the church. Dramatic stuff!

Well, I saw this so clearly, but what to do about it? We were totally unknown and Spring Harvest would hardly be interested in such novices. Yet surely God could open even such a door, somehow. . .

I had met the chairman, Colin Saunders, in July 1998 when visiting someone else (shortly after I'd received the Missions 2000 vision), and I had taken the opportunity to ask him if he would join a 'council of reference' we were putting together to underpin the missions. It had been a delightful encounter and he had said he would think about it. By October 1998, I was trying to finalise the council of reference and I tried to contact Colin's office. I got frustrated because that day he was in meetings and I couldn't get through. I prayed and asked the Lord to do something. That night, I was due to give an evangelistic talk to about 50 people at a dinner in a pub in Heathfield, a very small town in East Sussex. I did the talk, enjoyed it and was well received by the people. Several responded to the gospel and it was a very happy occasion – all the more so when the person who bounded up to me to thank me for my talk turned out to be none other than Colin Saunders, who happened to live in that town and had been invited to that dinner! I asked him there and then if he'd join the council of reference and he said he would. He gave me his home address and asked me to write to him. When I did so the next day, I wrote, 'This is what I would really like Spring Harvest to do for me. . .' and I explained the vision of me speaking and of the trumpeter. I even told him I had a trumpeter in mind (a team member from Canterbury). Well, as it happened, he knew the trumpeter too. And he was grabbed by the idea.

A few weeks later I heard from the chief executive of Spring Harvest that the proposal had already passed about five hurdles. They were minded to say 'yes', even though they had *never* provided a platform to promote events not directly associated with Spring Harvest, and he'd never seen such a proposal get this far. I was invited to address a key committee, shared the vision of the missions and what I had in mind – and they did indeed say 'yes'. The result? I did eleven main-stage presentations on two sites over three weeks around Easter 1999 (involving a massive amount of driving between Kent, Lincolnshire and North Wales) and presented the vision directly to about 23,500 people. At each presentation the key moment – the moment that people remembered years later – was when I asked the audience to stand and Kevin Kay-Bradley played his 'wake-up call', a trumpet solo which had a remarkable quality about it and which truly stirred the hearts of those present. In one city (Leeds), I later found out that a key church had decided not to participate in the On the Move mission, but changed its mind when 50 members of its congregation came back from Spring Harvest excited above all else about a vision for a free barbecue in the city centre in 2000! That church became the team base for the Leeds mission.

Meanwhile, we decided we had to move house. This was purely because the redundancy money from the TEC hadn't come and we couldn't afford to stay in a house with such a high mortgage. But what was the Lord doing here? Were we simply to move into a smaller house in the Maidstone area, or was a bigger move in order? We started to discern the voice of God telling us to move from Kent. I had the name 'Birmingham' in my mind. It made immense sense, as doing all these journeys from the centre of England would make the task not only much easier but, arguably, *possible*. We had met Revd John Hughes of St John's Harborne, Birmingham, at New Wine and loved him immediately. It was he who invited us to address the 50 pastors in the city and, on our way to see him prior to that meeting, we asked God to confirm to our hearts as we arrived in Birmingham whether that was the place for us. I had a distinct 'coming home' feeling as we got there and John himself, hearing that we were considering moving, said, 'Birmingham is a good place!'

Nonetheless, the idea of moving, which first came to us in September 1998, was not popular back home. Our vicar and his wife were adamant that it was a wrong move. A board member who had lived in Birmingham said it was a difficult society to break into. Some felt the move was the right thing. Others questioned whether we should move away from our 'support base' in Kent. Still others questioned whether we should uproot the children. Here, then, started an agonising period of heart-searching which carried on for several months. We seemed to receive only conflicting and confusing advice. To make it worse, our house wasn't selling. We didn't know what to do. It was most unsettling.

It was only in January 1999 that we came to a decision. I asked a delightful woman of prayer on the Springboard executive council to pray for God's guidance for us. She said, 'I'll look at Scripture. That's how I receive guidance from God.' One minute later she was back, all smiles. 'I just opened the Bible to hear from the Lord about you and this is where I opened it. You may find it significant.' It was the end of Luke 9, where Jesus encounters a number of men who make excuses as to why they can't follow him. He then says, 'Foxes have holes and the birds of the air have nests, but the Son of Man has nowhere to lay his head' (v. 58). We had felt we would be leaving our 'nest'. Then came the words, 'No-one who puts his hand to the plough and looks back is fit for service in the kingdom of God' (v. 62).

We resolved to spend a few days in Birmingham (someone, completely unasked, had offered us a house to stay in) and check it out, with the children. In particular, we wanted to go to a service at St John's. Our 'fleece' was that, if it was right, the children would love it. As it happened, the sermon was given that day (exceptionally) by the youth leader. They did love it. And the sermon was all about Joshua crossing the Jordan and moving to a new land.

We returned, resolved to move. Our house had been on the market for three months, generating no interest. The very next day after our return from Birmingham, having made our decision, our house sold. Interestingly, the couple who bought it told us that they hadn't actually been looking for a house, but when they saw the picture of ours in the estate agent's window they immediately fell in love with it, and for that reason alone made the decision to move house. Extraordinary.

Now sure of our decision, we went on a Saturday to tell our vicar Eric of our decision. He was sad, but accepting. He did say, however, that it would be good if the rightness of the decision could be independently confirmed. We agreed that it would be good.

The very next day, at the Sunday evening service, I persuaded Gina to go forward for ministry. (I am always up there, but Gina tends to be reluctant.) The speaker at that service was a pastor with a prophetic ministry. He saw Gina coming towards him and he declared to her, 'You've just turned a corner in your life.'

Gina said, 'Yes, we've just decided to move to Birmingham.'

'That's right,' he said. 'God is saying: that is the right decision.'

Eric, ministering to someone else nearby, was craning his

neck towards Gina and overhearing everything. Later he found us and said, 'OK – you're right; it's right for you to go.'

The prophet also said to Gina, 'The Lord is saying to you: don't settle for a house you don't like.' She was somewhat sceptical, as we had already discovered that we couldn't afford the kind of house in Birmingham we wanted, in the area we wanted.

In the end the sale of our house propelled us to move sooner than we had intended. The church gave us a lovely send-off and at the end of April the family moved – all except Cristina, who stayed with friends to complete her GCSE exams. We had to rent a small house for a season. I don't recommend renting (you're in such a weak position and it's difficult to feel at home), and I don't recommend trying to squeeze a big family into a small house. We had one L-shaped room downstairs which had to double up as our dining room, sitting room, piano room and office. The poor dog had nowhere to lie. I felt ever so claustrophobic and had to keep going for walks just to get out. Now, as a householder, I have more of a sense of how lucky we are and I feel for those less fortunate.

Anyway, this went on for three and a half months. Finally, we went to see a house that the estate agent swore would be suitable, even though we thought it looked pretty crummy from the outside. She was right and we were wrong. It was very suitable, spacious and – although the interior decor would have put people off as much as the outside – we could immediately see the potential. And an off-putting house is a cheap house! Thus we were able to buy a house which we could afford and which (after a little work) we would – and do – really like.

*   *   *

We did excellent town missions. We also had some encouragement about the missions of the previous year. The Baptist Union Research in Mission team had offered to do some research about the success or otherwise of the follow-up process. We had typically been collecting approximately 50 to 100 response cards on each mission (about a third of which might indicate that the guest had made a Christian commitment, two thirds saying that they wanted to know more). The research team decided to investigate what had happened subsequently to those people, after 6 to 9 months, based on a sample of 53 response cards held by 9 churches in 5 towns. Of this sample of 53 people, 19 were found to be still worshipping in those churches; 5 had lost touch; 6 had moved out of area; 9 had been referred to other churches; and the remaining 14 were still in touch. Thus, nearly 40 per cent had joined one of the nine churches, while some 80 per cent of the contacts were arguably still 'live'.

Having previously done only town missions, Leicester, a smallish city with about 300,000 people, was a perfect size for us to try out our first multi-site mission. The lessons learnt from this would be crucial for the city-wide missions the following year. Interestingly, the contact had come through Michael Green's newspaper article a year earlier.

We settled on three barbecue sites in Leicester in three sectors of the city. It was a very good mission. We had pastors from Kent with teams from their churches leading two of the sites (a model we would use extensively in 2000 and beyond), while Gina and I based ourselves in the city centre and visited the other sites.

The training evening, with about 500 team members present for all three sites, was exhilarating. The missions did well. Most crucially, a question was answered: what do we do if it rains?

In 37 days of mission to that point, it never had rained. Sometimes it had rained just before or just after the barbecue, but never on it! Now, on the third day of a four-day mission, it rained. The rain started at the beginning of the day and showed no sign of abating. Because there were three separate teams for three separate barbecue sites, each one had to make an immediate and independent decision about what to do. All three decided the same thing: move venue to the nearest and most appropriate church building or church hall; cook out of doors, under gazebos; worship on the streets in the rain, under umbrellas (a curious sight); funnel the people who came indoors to have their meals there. In each case, it worked. Probably fewer people came than would otherwise have come, but the atmosphere was great, and many commented on not having been inside a church for a long time – if ever.

*   *   *

As we had gone round making presentations in the various cities, I had often been reminded about the feeding of the five thousand – not so much because we were feeding people, but because of the job the disciples were given there. Jesus told them to organise the crowd – to make the people sit in groups of 50. They must have gone round grouping people in this way, without having any real idea what Jesus was going to do or how he was going to do it. Why should we sit in a group of 50? Well . . . you'll find out! Now *we* were finding ourselves doing something similar, organising churches in each big city into numbers of local groupings, ready to fulfil the vision for the following year and hold simultaneous free barbecues – but without having a clue where the equipment would come from or how it could be afforded, or how we could afford to employ the staff (or other resources) needed to deliver what we had promised. It was a venture of faith indeed, although the Lord did gradually start to pull together a staff team and even some of the money to pay them.

There was actually an acute disappointment on the financial front in October 1999. God knew that we needed staff and consequently the money for salaries. The good news was that we heard from a major grant-giving trust that they would help support the salaries of a young couple we were hoping could join us. Very much the fault of my own exalted expectations, the bad news was that the money pledged (generous a gift though it was) was a third of the amount I had expected. I had put too many of my expectation eggs in this one basket!

I went for a walk in the park and, dispirited by this 'bad' news, asked the Lord what I was to do now. This had been the charitable trust where we had the best contacts. Where should I turn now? As I was asking this question, an oak tree loomed before me. It was a huge tree, the distinctive thing about it being the extraordinary number of acorns all over it – thousands upon thousands of them. I had never seen an oak tree like it. And then I knew: '*That* is how your funding will be – based on thousands and thousands of small donations.' Which (with some vital exceptions) is how it has been ever since.

The young couple joined us that month; another young-ster with an evangelistic gift came in January; another with a wonderful anointing in worship arrived in late April, along with a secondee from another organisation. A Cana-dian with administrative gifting (and, for once, a bit of experience) completed the core team. It was a talented, albeit young, team – as long as one turned a blind eye to some adventurous spelling. . . At peak times, seven or eight of us would be crammed into an office (really a converted garage and utility room in our home) frankly adequate for little more than three or four.

On the day the final member of the team joined, about two days before the first mission, we had a prayer time together. Gina was suddenly in floods of tears. She was inconsolable. Finally, when she steadied herself and was able to speak, she said that she felt the Lord had just shown her that Satan was going to sift us, the team, 'like wheat'. It was essential that we should resist temptation and that we should pray for each other.

*   *   *

Everything was more or less in place. Groups of churches in each city had carried forward the vision as received at the first presentation, with the single exception of Sheffield, whose initial welcome and decision to participate was later rescinded by a decision not to take on what they feared would be too much, as they had the Luis Palau mission already that year – a sad moment. There were other sad moments, as some local areas that had seemed on the point of saying 'yes' changed their verdict to 'maybe next year'.

(Out of literally dozens of 'maybe next years', I think only one ever followed it up.) In Liverpool, exceptionally, four areas that had actually decided to do it changed their minds at the last moment, reducing our 'definite' tally from six to two. It can be a painful experience to carry a vision, to see it received with joy and then (at least from my perspective) to see it snatched away.

Nevertheless, what we had left constituted a huge mission. In all, 40 groups of churches in eight cities were eventually to undertake the mission, an eightfold increase on what we had done in any previous year, and a massive operation in terms of logistics, administration and continued inspiration. The missions were 'on' and they were undoubtedly big. Nonetheless, the constant 'will they, won't they?' teaser up to the last minute made it very difficult to plan or predict, and that led to a huge shock at the first mission – Manchester.

6

Into the Fire

Letters had been sent out to 700 registered team members for five sites in Greater Manchester. Because it had so nearly been twice as many sites (12 looked likely just three months before the mission), we had booked a big place for the training evening. It seemed reasonable, as no church could hold enough people for ten or so sites (potentially 1,500 team members). But with 700 registered for five, and the likelihood (judging by past experience) that only three quarters would turn up, it was already obvious that the hall seating nearly 2,000 would be massively too big, even though we had got it at a fifth of the normal cost. By then, however, there was nothing to be done but turn up and make the best of it.

Before the Manchester training evening, there was a glitch. The city council refused permission to hold a church's free barbecue *anywhere* in the city centre. This was especially poignant since not only had no other city declined permission, but Manchester city council themselves *had* permitted the 'Gay Mardi Gras' to use the very same public spaces we wanted to use, just weeks before.

And these were 'the churches of Manchester', about 50 of them participating, all denominations working together, that were being forbidden to stage this event.

A meeting of the church's network, bringing together about 50 pastors, looked at this and determined that such a decision was out of order. They also decided that we/they should be prepared to go ahead with or without permission. It was finally the Bishop of Manchester who saved the day by offering us the use of the cathedral as our team base and the cathedral gardens as the venue for the barbecue – a wonderful venue. But what we didn't know was that some of the churches, while going along with their colleagues' support for the mission, were at the same time advising their people that 'the mission's off'.

While the news of the breakthrough with the cathedral was sent out immediately, we were now in a situation where a number of churches were, at best, half in and half out. To make matters worse, the pastor who had agreed to be the local co-ordinator of the city centre site turned out not to have done the job that we were relying on him to do. This meant in particular that the £4,000 that had to be raised from participating churches to cover the cost of the food given out (we came for free, but the food was a gift from the local churches to their people) had not been raised and, at the last moment, we found ourselves having to underwrite three quarters of that substantial sum from our own meagre resources, putting us in serious financial difficulties.

So the training evening came. At least we were now *into* the missions, rather than just preparing for them as we had been for nearly two years. But that night, as team members filed into this huge hall, we gradually got the hang of the fact that there were nowhere near enough of them. Someone counted 163 people in this massive hall. Now that was a bit of a blow to one's pride, for sure. But, more than that, it was a challenge to the whole project's viability. How could we actually *do* five barbecues with maybe 30 or so team members for each, when we had never in the past done one with less than 70 and were more used to having twice that many? We just didn't think it could be done. But this was the training evening. Here was the team (what there was of it – but they had loyally turned up and were worshipping with gusto) and our hearts came to be more full of concern for them than for anything else. But what was the Lord saying? Could we go ahead?

It's a strange thing. I never got a clear answer to that question. But, for the 20 minutes of worship to kick the evening off, we had gathered around Nick, our worship leader, about 30 musicians from the general team, who had been asked to bring their instruments. So, with no practice to speak of, this motley crew filled the stage – guitarists, drummer, violins, flutes, keyboards, singers, etc. – and they led us in worship. The sound was absolutely glorious, in fact it was angelic. The instruments harmonised so beautifully and there was such a profound sense of God's presence in the worship that stopping the evening and abandoning the mission just didn't seem to be an option. And so I had the difficult task of going up there and giving my testimony about how I felt the Lord had called these missions into being, how we had prepared for two years and how we were now going to see the vision fulfilled – when all around us the apparent evidence of the vision's total failure was staring me in the face.

The evening went well (if one could just forget about the numbers – but the Holy Spirit has a way of filling a place) and people in fact left greatly encouraged. We ourselves left encouraged, bemused, questioning, somehow hopeful. In such circumstances, the Holy Spirit seems to give you a grace to carry on, almost untouched by the turbulence around you.

*   *   *

The first day of the mission did not bring us the hoped-for additional team members, turning up for the mission itself. It was pretty much the 'Gideon's army' that we had seen at the training evening – and it was this small force that we, and the various site leaders (from Kent, Leicester and Devon), had to send out after the morning meetings on five sites. Just sending them out was as difficult a thing as we have ever had to do. To cap it all, it was cold and windy and unwelcoming in every sense. Such a tiny team. . .

Gina and I went around and encouraged the various teams as well as we could. Particularly vulnerable was the city centre site, where a pastor and friend called Ian Jones had brought a team of 13 with him from Leicester and found just a dozen locals to help him (out of 300 available 'on paper'). And *not a single local leader* had turned up, not even the 'local co-ordinator'. It was quite shocking.

Yet the two or so worship bands that we managed to put together on each site again had such a clear anointing. The team members were wonderful. Then people began to turn up at the barbecues in reasonable numbers. God started touching people. Somehow the cooks managed to prepare

enough food for the multitudes. We found that it was possible to do an On the Move mission with 30 team members,
or even less. And people came to Christ. At the time of sharing afterwards the brave little teams were full of what God
had done.

Meanwhile, a journalist had phoned me on my mobile in
the late morning, to ask if we had heard that animal rights
demonstrators were on their way to disrupt the city centre
barbecue. Why? Because we were serving burgers! The fact
that we also offered veggie-burgers, leaving our guests to
choose, did not placate their desire to display indignation.
What to do? Team members got together and we prayed
that God would frustrate their plans. Later, after the barbecue was finished, two policemen turned up to tell us what
had actually happened. Apparently, they had escorted this
crowd of would-be protesters back and forth across the centre of Manchester, the protesters trying to locate the cathedral (not an easy place to miss, you might think!) but
somehow narrowly missing it and (the police told us) every
time they came near, mysteriously taking a wrong turn. In
the end they simply gave up and went home. 'I know what
you would put this down to – and it *was* quite extraordinary,' said one of the policemen.

There was one other problem. For Day Two I had placed
the secondee who was working for us (a young leader, we
felt) with Ian Jones in the city centre to help support Ian
and be his right-hand man, in the absence of the local co-
ordinator or even a single local pastor. The other four sites
had plenty of local leaders fully involved, and therefore
supporting Ian and his tiny team in the city centre was the
clear priority. It was the very least we could do. But the

secondee turned out not to be there when Gina and I came
to visit. That night we asked him where he had been. He
said he had been helping another member of staff, who was
sorting out the movement of equipment in a lorry we had
hired for the purpose. So we checked with that person to
see if he would be OK on his own, pulling in volunteers to
help him if necessary, and he assured us that he would be
and understood there was another priority for the person
who had been helping him. So I had to explain to the secondee how important it was that he stayed in the city centre. Only he could do that job, whereas humping gear was
something that anyone could do. But the next day we had
a repeat performance. The secondee was nowhere to be
seen at the city centre and it turned out that he was *again*
helping his colleague with deliveries. So I had to talk to him
quite sharply that night, saying that he *had* to follow my
lead; that it was my job to have an overview and take the
decisions about staff deployment. It was to no avail. He did
it again the following day, after which I spoke to him as
firmly as I knew how, stressing that he absolutely *must* do
what we were asking him to do. Yet again he ignored this
instruction.

We later learnt that the person he was helping was out of
his depth and couldn't cope. If only they had told us this,
we would have been able to do something about it. But, as
it was, an atmosphere of secrecy was keeping us out of the
counsel of our own staff members, with the intimation that
somehow we didn't (or wouldn't) *care*. Now, we were certainly overstretched ourselves, but we had always tried to
make it a priority to ensure that our core team was OK. . .
Anyway, I had to say to the secondee that I could not work

with him on this basis. He said that if I didn't want his help, I could do the missions on my own. There was the most awful confrontation with both him and the colleague he had been helping. With the former, we had to part company there and then. The latter restrained himself when we made it clear that we didn't have a problem with him and that he should not interfere. All this at the close of a mission – moments before the final celebration.

So, with a sense of dismay, this extraordinary quarrel still ringing in our ears, we made our way to St Anne's Church to join team members from all five sites to celebrate what God had done in the mission.

Actually, the mission had gone from strength to strength, although on one of the sites the numbers coming to the barbecue had been thin. But all the sites had testimony upon testimony about what God had done. Here are a few examples, to give a flavour.

Two men were invited to the barbecue. There they were so touched by the Lord that they both gave their lives to him. They then confessed why they had actually come to town that day. They had intended to commit burglary – yet they had, to their amazement, been drawn by God onto *his* agenda for that day, and for their lives.

A man from the supermarket who baked the bread for one of the missions came to check it out on the Saturday. His wife said she was an atheist, but didn't mind talking. She ended up giving her life to Christ and then proceeded to lead her own daughter to Christ too. The daughter led the younger brother to the Lord, after which all of them turned around to the father – who also asked Jesus into his life.

An older woman poured out her heart to a team member. He prayed for her and she was greatly impacted by Christ. But she had been hurt too many times for her to feel able to give her name and address. However, she asked him for his own name – which turned out to be her maiden name. Somehow touched by this, she opted to give her address after all – *but only for him*, because she trusted him.

One woman on the team prayed that she would lead someone to Christ. Minutes later she met an old schoolfriend, whom she hadn't seen since their childhood. They talked and prayed together, and she was able to lead her friend to Christ minutes before that lady had to leave for her home – in Holland.

A lady came to the barbecue with her twin grandchildren, one of whom had cerebral palsy. Her former husband, a church minister, had had an affair, after which she turned away from Christ. She came to the barbecue every day and finally recommitted her life to Christ. She said, 'During the four days, I got closer and closer to God.' She came to church on the Sunday and her grandchild was prayed for, for healing. The next day the child was seen by the consultant, who had previously said, 'She will never walk.' Now he said, 'This child will walk.' Three years on, we heard what had subsequently happened: the child was well and developing normally (just the same as its twin), and the family were members of a local church.

The security man at a local shopping centre came to the mission leader and said, 'Today has been the first crime-free day at the shopping centre that I've ever experienced.'

A team member took a bus to the final celebration. Seeing her 'On the Move Team Member' badge, a woman on the bus approached her to thank her for all she and the team had been doing – and explained that she had been to the barbecue and felt God touch her. She asked how she could find out more about Christianity and gave her name and address so that she could be contacted.

And so on. As people were served with free food, and as the church came out and worshipped and extended the hand of friendship to strangers, God was able to move miraculously and 83 people that we know of – plus, no doubt, a whole lot more that we don't – gave their lives to Christ on the streets, and hundreds gave their names and addresses because they wanted to know more. The tiny team had seen as much fruit as teams five times that size usually did, and the divine appointments and miracles of grace were too numerous to keep track of. Even the weather had been lovely after a difficult Day One; and, interestingly, we have seen more Manchester team members helping in other towns and cities subsequently than team members from any other city.

*   *   *

Liverpool saw a wonderful mission, with a slightly bigger team – helped considerably by pastors and team members coming across, at short notice, from Manchester to help. Subsequently, team members and pastors from there joined us at the next venue, Leeds. There, joy of joys, we had nearly 400 team members at the training evening to staff four barbecue sites, and real church unity underpinned the evangelism just as it underpinned the organisation of the mission. It was the best mission yet and seemed to open a door on a new phase. The agony of the first mission (along with God's undoubted intervention) was replaced by joy in unity and in the privilege of ministering to the multitudes. The final celebration in St George's Church was a revelation in itself – a taste of heaven, as we worshipped and thanked and celebrated. One extra thing in all of our hearts was that apparently this was the first time in anybody's memory that the black and white churches in Leeds had worked together in mission. I think the black churches greatly enjoyed the recognition of their massive contribution to the mission, and the rest of the team welcomed the feel and style of that contribution with glee. What a church we can be when we are one! Three of the Birmingham sites a few weeks later were led by Leeds pastors and teams.

Missions followed in Nottingham, Bristol and then Birmingham, which was the biggest mission so far, on seven sites. For Gina and me, excellent missions in each area were combined with concern about the growing militancy of the animal rights people, who had contrived to come to each mission. How had they known where we would be? Well, someone had suggested a couple of months before the missions that I really should seek some press coverage, as there would be people who would love to take part but wouldn't know it was happening. I contacted the *Christian Herald* and the result was a big splash taking up the whole front page, headed 'Burger Kings'! They gave the dates of each mission in the series. The animal rights activists had somehow seen it and resolved to sustain a nationwide campaign against what we were doing. I actually felt rebuked by the Lord for *seeking* press coverage in this way. The fruit had been bitter. Far better to take the press coverage which he gave us, which had been considerable, without trying to manufacture it. We've kept to that policy ever since.

The weakest – but most remarkable – site in Birmingham was Handsworth, a poor area populated by Asians, West Indians, Vietnamese, Chinese, Iranians and people from many other nations. The local churches had welcomed the mission, but it turned out, on a quick check two days before the mission, that they hadn't actually applied to the council for permission to hold the event. This normally takes months. I phoned up the main Birmingham council switchboard and explained the problem. 'You need Highways,' I was told. The woman put me through and I found myself talking to another woman. 'Oh, I know about the free barbecue initiative. I go to the New Testament Church of God in Handsworth.' She said that, somehow, within two hours, she would have permission from the council, the police and the fire brigade. 'I am trusting and believing,' she said. She was as good as her word. The approval from the fire brigade was just as well, because when the diminutive team got there for Day One of the mission, they found that the ground had not been prepared and was about two inches deep in pigeon droppings! It was the fire brigade who saved the day by offering to come and hose down the site for us.

One team member, buying disinfectant for the site, was asked by the pharmacist what it was to be used for. She explained about the Christian event, which was to take place across the road. The man, a Sikh, went white. He said to the team member that he'd had a dream two days before, in which he saw a Christian event happening on that very spot. He was clearly quite emotional, and in a way anxious, about the fact that it was now happening as he had seen it in his dream. The impact of the mission on this man's family was profound. By the end of three days of mission, two members of his immediate family had given their lives to Christ.

Seventeen people, nearly all Muslims, Sikhs and Hindus, gave their lives to Christ in three lunchtimes there. One man looked at the scene – it was raining, two thirds of the seats were empty and there were still pigeon droppings nearby – and said, 'You'll never get Utopia here on earth, but this is the nearest thing to it I've ever seen.' A remarkable comment, so revealing of what the Lord himself was doing there, for it was surely only the move of the Spirit that made the place 'attractive'. Another man, a Sikh, said to me, 'You people are giving away free food; you are doing it in the rain; you people have good hearts.' Minutes later, with tears running down his face, he gave his life to Christ – and was taken under the wing (through a dream, that night) of another Christian man with a Sikh background.

*   *   *

All this remarkable ministry was coinciding with a rather more strained position at our base. The issue of having to part company with the secondee at the beginning of the Manchester mission had left a seed of resentment with one or two; and although the whole staff team worked extremely hard to the finish, and while some members were as good as gold and remain close friends, it was clear that our unity as a whole team had been affected. Gina and I prayed, we communicated with all concerned as best as we could, but there was something that we couldn't quite reach. We were very aware of Gina's 'word' at the beginning that Satan was going to sift us like wheat – and that the open row had taken place just days later. There was a feeling of pain in our hearts, even while the ministry on the streets was proving spectacular and the churches could hardly contain their excitement.

We were also low on money (mainly because of the Manchester fiasco) and our board of trustees started getting concerned about that one – another seeming contradiction with the freedom and joy experienced on the streets. At this point we also lost another of the ten cities. Stockton-on-Tees actually did the mission years later, but at this point were refused permission by the local council.

So we experienced disappointment and anxiety, mixed in with breakthrough. Newcastle at the end of July produced one of the best missions, again underpinned by a beautiful unity. The London mission was much the biggest, with 15 groups of churches in 15 areas of London doing mission simultaneously, generously led by 15 church leaders, with accompanying teams, from around the UK.

The reason so much practical support was given in this way was that people, pastors and ordinary team members alike, *saw God moving*. They wanted more, and they wanted to be part of that more. Here are some examples from that year's missions.

A young woman from Australia, as she refused an invitation to a free barbecue for the fourth time, apparently heard an 'audible voice' in her head saying, 'You've come halfway around the world to find something, and this is it!' She stopped dead in her tracks and asked the team member,

'Who *are* you?' – to which the team member innocently replied that she was part of a group of churches putting on a free barbecue for the community. The young woman decided to come to the team member's church the next morning, where somebody quite different led her to Christ.

A pastor listened to a shopkeeper who insisted on relaying his philosophy of life, which was both boring and baseless. But when the pastor was minded to interrupt and turn the conversation 'his way', he felt the Holy Spirit say, 'Just shut up and listen!' (or words to that effect). So he did, wondering where this was going. After nearly half an hour of this, the man changed tack and enquired of the pastor whether he had heard about the young man who had been murdered nearby, a fortnight before. The pastor confirmed that he had – it had been big news. 'That was my son. . .' Suddenly the man dissolved into grief and the pastor found himself ministering to a broken heart.

A team member prayed for healing for a woman whose back was causing her great pain. She returned to the barbecue the next day and asked to be allowed to speak at the microphone. This non-Christian lady then explained to everyone at the barbecue site that she had been prayed for and that as a result she had enjoyed the first pain-free 24 hours in 20 years.

Another woman on the team spoke to an elderly lady who was lonely following the death of her husband six months previously. The team member suggested that they might go into the church and read the Bible together, and the lady greeted this idea warmly. When they finally parted, the lady said, 'A few days ago, God showed me in a dream that he was going to send an angel to comfort me. The minute I saw you on the high street, I knew that you were the angel that he was sending me.'

Sometimes people suggest that we should do things like role play in the training evenings, the better to teach how to do evangelism. My strong instinct has always been to resist that, based on what we have consistently seen the Lord actually doing, again and again, on the streets. None of these stories are based on our team members being particularly 'good' at what they are doing; they are about the sovereign move of God. If we ever got 'expert' at what we do, I believe that more of our ministry would tend to mean less of his. The key, I believe, is to go out with the right heart, a radical sense of our own weakness and dependence on the Lord. Then he is free to act. And he does!

Another, rather different, highlight concerned a local gang leader, who enjoyed sitting at the city centre barbecue each day, not letting anyone talk to him but seemingly drinking in the worship nonetheless. When the animal rights demonstrators got over-boisterous, he got up and walked towards them. With all the menace he could muster (and he scored high on the menace stakes, believe me), he said to them, 'What these people here are doing is good. If you interfere, I'm going to knock your lights out.' The animal rights group slunk back. Should we Christians approve? Maybe not, but inwardly, I feel sure, we all thought, '*Yeah*!'

*   *   *

Actually, the missions had left us broke. We were facing a deficit of at least £10,000 by the end of the year. One or two of the trustees were very concerned, but we need not have worried. 'God pays for what he orders,' and when we mailed our backlist of team members at the end of the missions, donations totalling £25,000 flooded in.

There was no deficit. But was there a future? The big vision had been fulfilled. Was there to be anything next? There was surely no point just carrying on for the sake of it.

7

A Call to the Nations

It was actually early in 1998, our first year of OTM, that Gina had a flash of insight in the Spirit. She said, 'I can see us on a plane. I think we're going to do a lot of flying. No – really *a lot of flying.*' Little did we know how true that would be. But it was only now, after some months of asking for clarification from God about what should follow Missions 2000, that the Lord started revealing his plans for us.

We had thought of closing OTM down. Not that we didn't think it was worth continuing – only that, having had such a clear focus for the previous two years, it seemed odd and altogether inappropriate just to carry on with no apparent steer for the future. We so much wanted to hear from God.

That steer came at the beginning of November 2000. We were still pretty exhausted. But we came to worship one morning, as a diminutive staff team (most had just been taken on for the missions in 2000), and it happened when we were singing 'Shine, Jesus, Shine'. We got to the chorus, where it says, 'Flood the nations with grace and mercy,' and

I distinctly heard God say, 'Today, you *own* an international calling.'

The song finished and I shared what I felt I had heard. Gina said, 'It's funny you should say that. During the song I was reminded of the thought you had about 30 capital cities.' It had been more of a daydream than a vision, about a year previously, while we were driving to a meeting in London. I had said then that I wondered if the Lord was saying we should look to do missions in the 30 major capital cities of the world in 2005. It had seemed too daft for words and the idea had not been mentioned in a year. Now, during the song, it had come back to Gina. And, as she said this, one of the two most profound spiritual experiences of my life happened, there and then. Just as in 1998, when the heavy weight had come on my shoulders and I had received the vision for Missions 2000, once again a heavy weight came on my shoulders, if anything, more intensely than the first time. Now, there are some experiences that you just can't contrive. The intensity of this one was almost unbearable – a heavy pressing down, which continued unabated for some minutes. I knew that God was saying, 'Yes, this is what I want you to do.' It was a vision on an extraordinary scale, but I knew without a doubt that I had heard God. If so, it surely *could* be accomplished.

The experience subsided. Remembering the business with the spare car in 1998, I thought we should ask for confirmation. I said to the others, 'Let's ask God to confirm this through a letter in today's post.' That was agreed. Now, our postbag is very seasonal. In July we might get 30 letters in a single post, but in November we'd be lucky to get one. On this occasion there was indeed just one. I opened it with some trepidation. Was it a gas bill (the kind that drove our accountant apoplectic, because every quarter we had to tell British Gas that we didn't actually use gas at the warehouse. . .)? Was it an invitation to take out another credit card? Well, no it wasn't. God was kind to us. It was a letter from the leader of a Christian worship band from London, which had travelled to play in the missions in Leeds and Nottingham. He wrote simply to say, 'I believe God is saying that your ministry will be both near and far.' It was significant that this should come on that particular day. Then he gave a Scripture and that was even more significant: 'A little yeast permeates the whole lump of dough' (Galatians 5:9).

Immediately, that Scripture struck me powerfully and in two ways. First, the lump of dough was the world and, yes, a tiny ingredient (which yeast is) could influence the whole thing. Second, there was something about the *character* of the yeast. After all, no-one ever sees or tastes bread and says, 'What wonderful yeast!' The yeast is a hidden ingredient, whose purpose is to help the bread *to be bread*. In the same way, On the Move should work in a low-profile way, helping the church to be the church – so that what you saw at the end of the process was not OTM, but the local church. Indeed, as the yeast helps the bread to rise, it was time for the church to 'arise'. We were to be a yeast, acting as a catalyst to that process.

We knew we had received our confirmation. When we put it to the trustees, not for the first time they responded by saying, 'This sounds really exciting!' – as opposed to 'This is daft!' or 'Where would we get the money from?' or any of the other reasonable enough responses they might have made. By the end of 2000, three out of four members of the board were stepping down (having joined essentially for a Kent and Sussex phase!) and new people joined to serve alongside Kerry Thorpe, who became our second chairman. We were able to choose trustees with the 2005 challenge in mind. At least in terms of our inner orientation, the missions project for 2005 was launched.

*   *   *

It was from that moment of envisioning, almost to the day, that waves of attack started. I don't want to go into detail on most of it and some of it can't be divulged in a book at all. But readers need to know that, for the next year or so, we suffered a series of attacks from the Enemy that went way beyond our expectations in terms of their ferocity and unremitting nature.

There was a pastor we learnt very bad things about. What do you do with such information? What made the matter more urgent was that he was focusing on young and vulnerable people. We confronted him with what we knew and warned him not to continue his activities with local youngsters. He agreed – but didn't in fact stop. What to do now? We reluctantly decided to tell two key individuals what we knew, and they were most grateful. But the pastor concerned started speaking against us in all sorts of ways as a result. Very unpleasant.

Quite separately, one of our children suffered sexual abuse – and this from a 'Christian', someone connected to On the Move. This, in Shakespeare's words, was 'the unkindest cut of all'.

Separately again, On the Move found itself being the victim of fraud, as someone forged a form supposedly written by me, in order to gain an insurance payout. And there was more.

Now, Psalm 34:19 says, 'Many are the afflictions of the righteous; but the LORD delivers him out of them all' (RSV). The Lord did deliver us from each of them, wonderfully. Things that were hidden got exposed; the Lord provided vindication for us when we needed it – out of the blue, it seemed, albeit after some time. Our child who suffered abuse was delivered amazingly and completely, with full healing – and went forward the stronger for it. But one cannot deny that those experiences were deeply painful. We knew that the key to surviving such attacks was always to forgive anybody that hurt us. Sometimes we had to do so again and again, as anger and resentment, which we thought we had dealt with, would resurface. All this can be hard work! I thank God that Gina and I had each other and also some dear friends who supported us and ministered to us. But it was a 'bloody' time. It did take its toll. We felt embattled and wondered when it might end.

It wasn't to end, yet. There was more to come – some of the most frightening episodes yet. But such experiences provide an opportunity for God to show his power. Here is one instance in which we certainly needed him to do so. If he didn't, we would lose everything – our house, our ministry, the lot.

*   *   *

You may recall that we were now fighting for £30,000, after Kent TEC (the Chamber's merger partner) agreed to settle with me for that sum – and then went back on that deal too. That 'agreement' had come in June 1998 and we had started court proceedings shortly afterwards. But legal wheels turn slowly. In fact, the issue was finally scheduled to come to court in December 2000, but the night before we were informed that the case was postponed because they couldn't find a judge! And so it was that a new court date was set, the 7th June 2001.

The only problem was that at the end of May 2001 our solicitor friend – who was acting for us for free – resigned from his firm of solicitors (following a fracas there) and transferred to a new job elsewhere. No longer being a partner of 'our' firm of solicitors meant that, just one week before our court action, he had lost the authority to write off the costs of the work he'd been doing for us over three years. The result? A snotty letter from the senior partner of our firm telling us that, while we might have understood that the work was being done for us for free, this was not the case. Including the forthcoming hearing itself, the cost of the legal work they had done for us would amount to . . . wait for it . . . £95,000.

On the 1st June we met our barrister for the first time. He was an excellent man and we had full confidence in him. Only, he told us that we would lose. Our weakness was that the evidence we did now have in writing all post-dated the actual agreement. In law you need something 'contemporaneous' to show what happened, rather than a subsequent account (e.g. in a letter), which can only demonstrate that the writer *thought* something had happened – not that it actually had. So, while our case was morally compelling, these things were not decided in moral terms, but according to the letter of the law.

So this was the picture: if we did lose, we would be responsible for paying £95,000 to our solicitors and perhaps an equivalent amount to the other side to cover their legal costs. If we won, we would get £30,000. Losing would mean losing our house and possible bankruptcy. And we were now being told by our own barrister that we would, in fact, lose.

During that meeting with the barrister, I said I wanted to tell him an anecdote – that when we first considered the action, I had asked God to guide me through the Scripture verse in that day's *Times*. I passed him over the copy of the newspaper and he read the verse, which you'll remember said, 'I, the LORD, will appear before you in court, quick to testify against sorcerers, adulterers and perjurers, against those who cheat the hired labourer of his wages' (Malachi 3:5). He looked up and said, 'That's either absolutely amazing, or a very sick joke.' With that, the meeting ended.

Two days before the proceedings, we had a phone call from our solicitors. They were well aware of our predicament and they had also come to realise that Kent TEC didn't want the publicity that would come from the court action going ahead. It might be possible to negotiate a deal whereby everybody 'walked away'. We'd have to forgo our £30,000, but the TEC would pay their own costs and most of ours without admitting guilt, while our solicitors might write off the rest (fearing that if we went bankrupt, they wouldn't see it all anyway). We could potentially walk away scot-free. This was a very attractive proposition.

Gina and I sat on the terrace overlooking our back garden that Tuesday afternoon to discuss what we should do. It was actually our children who rallied round at that point and gave us their perspective. God had said that he would appear before me *in court,* and it would be *disobedient* for us not to take it to court now. Have you ever had your arm bent up behind your back in a half nelson to make you submit? It was difficult to resist their simple logic. Then our youngest, Nicholas – aged 11 – said, 'I think God wants you to look at page 653 of the Bible.' He just had that figure in his mind. He had said something similar just two days before, and it had been bang on. So we looked it up. It was Psalm 74, which starts by saying how awful everything is, then says to the Lord that he can do anything, and then comes the key verse. It says, 'Arise, O God, plead your cause' (v. 22). It was this use of legal language that convinced me. God was indeed saying that we should bring it to court and we simply had to be obedient. Imagine the surprise of the solicitors when we phoned to say that we were taking it to court after all. '*You are*?'

The first day in court went OK. The second was more dramatic. In the afternoon, I had a vision. I guess I shouldn't have been surprised, as the Scripture verse promised specifically that 'I will appear before you in court'. Well, he did! I saw, behind the judge's bench, but five times larger than the judge, the figure of the Lord Jesus, seated on a throne, holding a sceptre and wearing a crown. Strangely, it was a black-and-white image. I guess it was in my mind. But I saw this consistently over three hours. And, over three hours, I turned many times to confer with my solicitors, and Gina and I spoke to each other – and I would forget. But every time I looked *there*, there it was. It was clearly located in one place in the courtroom.

While this was going on in the spiritual realms, what was

going on in the natural was clearly impacted by it. Precisely during that three-hour period, the two key witnesses of the other side were being cross-examined. And they made an absolute hash of it. They contradicted themselves and each other, and were obviously lying. I found it staggering to see the impact of Jesus' presence in the courtroom on those who weren't even aware of it. They may indeed not have been aware of it, but they were being massively *affected* by it. Their case just fell apart and I have never seen two people looking so uncomfortable!

After the hearing was adjourned for the day, we met the barrister for a short debrief. He said, 'I know it has gone fantastically today, but don't get too excited: you will still lose for the reasons that I explained.' But I *was* excited. I went home that Friday night and told everybody (to Gina's horror), 'We're going to win!' and, 'I saw the Lord in the courtroom!' I was not only excited; I was quite sure.

By Tuesday morning, however, when the case resumed, we were rather less sure. The judge seemed to be bending over backwards to agree with the points the other side were making. One of their two key witnesses, their solicitor who had made the deal, was again being cross-examined and was now making a much better fist of it. Gina and I went for a walk in the park during the tea break. We felt gloomy and downcast and turned to prayer. We said, 'Lord, even if we lose, we will still serve you. . .' and other prayers to that effect. We then returned to face the music.

Judge Green returned and, without warning, started to deliver his judgement, whereby the judge tells the story, as he has come to understand it, of what 'really happened'. 'This is good,' we began to think. Throughout the trial, he had sometimes seemed not fully to grasp much of what was being said, but now it transpired that he had grasped everything. We couldn't have hoped for a more luminous retelling of what had really happened. And all the while that he was delivering his judgement, I had another vision. This time it was a large sceptre, positioned diagonally (just as it had been on the Friday, in the hands of the Lord Jesus) behind the judge's bench. There it stayed for the full 20 minutes or so that it took for the judgement to be delivered. As the judgement proceeded, it turned out that, on the previous day, which he had taken as a 'reading day', the judge had himself found a brand-new precedent (Anglian Water versus Railtrack), in which that judge had ruled that in certain circumstances things written after the agreement *could* be taken as evidence. It was on this basis that he was able to find 'in favour of the claimant' – and that was me!

Thank you, Lord! There were hugs in the courtroom, massive relief and joy. We soon joined the two representatives from our firm of solicitors and the barrister in the tea room. They looked up as we approached them and one of them said, 'We have just been discussing the amazing things we have seen in the courtroom. It has been a real road to Damascus experience for all of us.' Apparently, some weeks later, the legal team themselves got together specifically to celebrate this signal victory.

It later occurred to us that, had the case gone to court the previous December as planned, the new precedent would not yet have been set. I also investigated the significance of the sceptre. Psalm 45:6 says, 'A sceptre of justice will be the sceptre of your kingdom.' I could have wept when I read that, and could now as I write it.

*   *   *

The other trouble that came upon us concerned our first international mission. In retrospect, one might imagine that it would be heavily contested by the Enemy. It certainly was.

Sometimes, Satan's strategies can be advanced through people who have no awareness that they are figures on a bigger canvas. In fact, it all started with the best intentions, as one of the cities in England where we had done missions in 2000 decided that it would be good to serve their twin city on the continent by taking the mission there, with our hands-on help and involvement. It was actually a wonderful mission, but this helped persuade a local leader that he should take On the Move across that country, even though we hadn't asked him to do so. He was an Englishman (which didn't seem ideal for leading OTM in a foreign country) and, more to the point, we simply didn't feel that he was the right person to do so. There was a clear 'no' in our hearts. But was our reluctance really as a result of hearing from God, or was it a case of 'Martin won't let go'?

Gina never had any doubts. She was quite clear that he was not the right person. But, once I was challenged about my reactions, I subjected myself to merciless self-analysis as to my true motives and, although I always came to the same conclusion – that he wasn't the right person – I managed to make myself suffer inordinately over the issue. I had literally months of anguish, in which I now had to handle the fact that this person had decided he would do it anyway, and also the fact that our own board was deeply concerned and deeply divided about what was going on here and who was really at fault. Everyone wanted to do the right thing.

But the piggy in the middle, with his motives and heart under the microscope, was me. I found this so hard. It evoked deep things in my character and in my past. I was being severely undermined by it all and started to develop physical symptoms to go with my emotional turmoil.

Then the Lord himself did something. As part of the unfolding international strategy, we had distinctly heard the Lord tell us to go to an international conference of about 2,000 people from 68 nations, taking place in Hanover, Germany. It was from that conference, directly or indirectly, that the contacts for our first few international missions all came. But, while we were there, one of our trustees, Robert Ward, took me (at Gina's behest) to Cindy Jacobs, a speaker at the conference and a noted prophet from the USA, to ask her to pray for me. 'It's very strange,' she discerned as she started praying for me. 'I get very strongly the words. . .' And there she spoke God's words to me, uncannily describing what had happened, clearly giving me God's perspective on it, showing me his love and affirmation and putting my mind completely at rest about what I had feared within myself. It was a seminal moment. I knew what God himself was saying, and so did one of my trustees who was there to hear the prophecy. God is good!

This problem had undermined; ultimately, it built up. I can honestly say that I developed a new confidence about who I am in Christ, about the authority he has given me and about our responsibility before God to nurture the vision with which he has entrusted us. We learnt about the kind of issues that would come up when we operated in a new country. It was a fast learning curve, and one which has stood us in good stead in subsequent years. Painful, though!

*   *   *

With the first international mission under our belts, and lots of interest from other countries for further missions, it was clear that we would need help in combining the twin tasks of developing the international ministry and keeping the UK side going in a meaningful way. We had completed a number of good missions in 2001, particularly a London-wide initiative across 14 sites and major missions in Southampton and Coventry. But 2002 was looking to be a busy year both at home and abroad. We therefore appointed a lovely Scotsman, Mike Stewart, to be our Head of UK Mission. He joined from the 1st January 2002, and actually had his first day with us on the 2nd. We had an excellent day together dreaming about what we would do, who would do what, and so on – and then he went home. The next morning, his wife phoned us at 8.00 a.m. 'I have something really awful to tell you . . . Mike died last night.'

Mike was actually sitting in his kitchen back home with his wife Trina, at the end of his first day with us. Out of the blue, and with no previous history of such a thing, he had a heart attack and died.

Trina was incredibly strong and courageous. The funeral in Coventry, attended by over 400 people who had been blessed through Mike's life and ministry, was a most moving occasion.

Gina and I were shattered by the news. We had grown to love Mike in the two years we had known him before he joined us; we felt desperately concerned for Trina and the kids; we wondered what it all meant for On the Move; and we wondered (who wouldn't?) what such an event could signify. Lord, what does this mean? Are you saying some-thing? Is this a terrible attack?

A couple of things helped us get some sort of a handle on what had happened; things that comforted us, and Trina too. One was that, as soon as the news had sunk in, we remembered the Bible passage that Gina and I had read with Mike the previous day, on his first and only morning with us. I had just had a name and number reference in my mind (Philippians 1) and when I looked it up and read the chapter, I had read aloud these verses of Paul's letter:

> I eagerly expect . . . that . . . Christ will be exalted in my body, whether by life or by death. For to me, to live is Christ and to die is gain. If I am to go on living in the body, this will mean fruitful labour for me. Yet what shall I choose? I do not know! I am torn between the two: I desire to depart and be with Christ, which is better by far; but it is more necessary for you that I remain in the body. . .

I read this to Mike on the day he died. His comment to us was, 'What a wonderful place to be.'

8

Learning the Ropes

W e gradually came to terms with what had happened. There was a full series of missions in
Britain and abroad being organised for 2002,
which we would somehow have to handle without the
expected help.

Terribly hard though the previous year had been, there
was one thing bringing us new joy. Nick Hoult, our worship
leader during 2000, proposed that February to our eldest
daughter Cristina – and she said 'yes'. I really think it was a
gift from God to bring us something truly positive at this
point and let us begin to focus on a very happy family occasion coming up in the summer. And it was, as it were, the
harbinger of a generally lighter and happier period of our
lives. Excellent missions took place and 12 of that year's 16
missions subsequently did it again within two years – a
heartening statistic. But the greatest developments were on
the international front.

Spain was a revelation, in that a very marginalised evangelical church in a historically Roman Catholic country had
been able to set up shop in the centre of the community and

welcome hundreds to a free meal. This brought a kind of breakthrough, which wouldn't have been needed in quite the same way in Britain, but was central to what the church needed there. For the first time, they – the local church – were being *received* by their own community. Evangelism, normally almost impossibly difficult there, was so easy that one local boy, aged twelve and helped by an adult, brought five adults to the Lord in two lunchtimes! The local leader said afterwards that in his 17 years of ministry there, they had tried 'everything' evangelistic and nothing had worked. This was the first time he had seen something that had really worked. Our UK team of nine was a delight and the Lord forged us into a joyous worship band (there were not enough local musicians), which really 'went some' during the mission.

Thanks to another Hanover contact, we also visited Nigeria in April to discuss the possibility of doing a mission there, in Port Harcourt, a major city on the coast. Now, this was something else! From the dingy, dirty hotel we had to stay at in Lagos on the way, to the food that seemed to burn a hole in my mouth, to the seven-hour car ride dodging potholes between Lagos and Port Harcourt, we were finding ourselves in unknown territory.

Gina had felt the Lord give her Isaiah 58 as the key Scripture to bring to the Nigerian church. This talks about the 'true fasting' (or, more loosely, one might say 'true religion'), which is really about looking after the needy. If you 'spend yourselves on behalf of the hungry', if you 'break every yoke', if you 'provide the poor wanderer with shelter' and 'loose the chains of injustice', then, it says, '*your* light will break forth like the dawn, and your healing will quickly appear; then your righteousness will go before you, and the glory of the LORD will be your rear guard. Then you will call, and the LORD will answer' (vv. 6–9).

The key impact of these verses in Nigeria was connected to the fact that the Lord had shown us that, when we went out internationally, we should charge nothing. Our time and our expenses should be a gift from the church in the UK. But, conversely, the local churches should pay for the food given out at the barbecue, because that was to be *their* gift to their people. And that was the problem. No-one, they told us, had *ever* asked them to pay for their own mission before. Normally, people would come from the West offering to pay for everything. Their job was just to turn out the people. For the first time, a Western ministry was telling them that they had to pay for the food (as a matter of principle) and was bringing Isaiah 58 as a word from the Lord. They decided that it was actually about time they paid for their own mission and took responsibility in this way. In their hearts, they did feel that the Lord was telling them truly to care for those outside the church (pastors there have a high status and they can be pretty bossy!) – and they agreed. We set dates for November 2002, and promised to come back with a team.

*　　*　　*

The mission itself was a revelation. The training evening saw us with about 30 pastors and 200 team members. I almost choked with emotion when I saw 200 Nigerian church members wearing the 'On the Move Team Member' badges, which we had been so used to seeing in the context of British missions. Two members of the UK group of ten (which mainly consisted of pastors) independently felt God saying that morning that we should wash the feet of the Nigerian pastors at the training evening. The English had taken advantage of their country and then left it to fend for itself when it no longer suited us to stay. We needed to say 'sorry'. We had originally come in many respects with a heart of arrogance, and now we needed demonstrably to come with a servant heart – and also to model that servant heart to the local Christians ahead of the mission.

Gina also came that evening with a prophetic word for the pastors. She felt so strongly that God was saying something, but we were not given the opportunity to share it – until the training evening itself. She told them that she had seen in her mind a picture of God sweeping the floor with a broom made of twigs. She asked him, 'What are you sweeping, Lord?'

He said, 'I am sweeping away the pastors who are not walking in holiness and who haven't been looking after my people.'

She said to the pastors, 'God is saying: unless you change your ways, he is going to sweep you away and raise up new pastors who are willing to do this.'

Then she saw God sweeping again and asked, 'Lord, what are you sweeping now?'

He said, 'I am sweeping away the government, which is not walking in holiness. I am tired of them abusing my children and I am raising up a new government that will care for them.'

Gina spoke with extraordinary authority and asked the people to intercede for the government. This was not an easy word to deliver to pastors who had invited us to come and do mission with them, let alone to deliver it on the eve of the mission and in front of all the people. But this word was received.

Then we explained how we wanted to wash the pastors' feet and, having come equipped with buckets, towels and water, proceeded to do so. It was such a moving 20 minutes or so, as the UK team did this. There was literally not a dry eye in the place (our team included) and, as one of the pastors later said, 'Something broke in the heavenlies that evening; I don't understand it, but something was broken in the spiritual realm and it was very significant.'

A year later we heard from a Kenyan prophet that exactly the same prophecy, of the Lord sweeping, had been given all over Africa. And did we know about the elections in Nigeria? They took place in January 2003, a few weeks after Gina gave the prophecy. The Nigerian government had been 'swept away!', to be replaced by a new one; and the new president was a committed Christian, who had only stood for office after two prophets had independently come to him to tell him that God was asking him to stand.

The mission itself in Port Harcourt was really a further expression of the move of the Spirit which started at the training evening, with the prophecy, the foot-washing, the tears and the love. People came in big numbers and felt especially touched in their hearts to hear that the food had been paid for by the pastors of the local churches (rather than by the visiting English team). They felt cared for and valued, and the result was that not only did waves of up to 100 at a time come forward to give their lives to Christ (an amazing 1,500 in three evenings), but the follow-up was later hailed by local leaders as excellent, following very poor experiences with some 'crusade' missions in the past – apparently because this time people felt loved and wanted to join the kind of churches that truly cared for the people.

Another highlight was when we asked at our hotel if we could pray for the staff, who had served us so faithfully. All 15 members of staff lined up for us in their red uniforms. David, a vicar travelling with us, gave them a simple presentation of the gospel and, with all eyes closed, asked them to raise a hand if they had just asked Jesus into their lives. All 15, with bowed heads, lifted their hands. We then prayed for each one individually. When we left the hotel, we were looked on with such love by all the staff – a most moving experience.

There was one close call, though. When we first announced at the barbecue that the food was ready, nobody moved! What was going on? Maybe the locals were too proud to be seen queuing up for free food. A slightly anxious 20 minutes passed – and during that time, dusk fell. Gradually, the locals became more than happy to queue up to get their rice and barbecued 'cow meat' under cover of darkness. Relief! The next day, of course, we waited till dark before we announced the meal. And to think that we had nearly opted, not for an evening meal, but for a lunchtime mission!

*   *   *

Into 2003 we prepared for further missions abroad – in Lyon, France, in Mostoles, Spain, and in Bielefeld, Germany. We also undertook a north of England mission, based in 14 towns across the far north – from York to Newcastle, Lancaster to Carlisle and much in between – as a response to a call I felt I had received from God the previous year. Although 14 towns seemed and was a large number, in my heart I had been hoping and striving for twice that number. And striving was probably the right word. Part of learning the ropes that year was to learn how to pursue a vision in a spirit of rest and trust, rather than having too much personal investment hanging on the uptake or otherwise of a vision which I believed was from God. This was to stand me in good stead for the vision for 2005. Trying to do *that* in a spirit of striving would have been a killer – both of the vision and of me!

The mission in Lyon was wonderful. Again, a marginalised evangelical church found itself at the centre of the community (in a highly prominent location in France's second city). Even the mayor turned out to 'bless' the event. The church (about 200 team members from 14 churches) was received by the people; the people in turn were wooed by the worship and there was, as it says in Acts 8, 'joy in that city'. An *On y Va* (literally 'Let's Go') organisation, joined with the wider OTM, has grown out of that mission.

The mission in Spain was on a smaller scale, with just two churches participating. But the Spirit certainly moved: some 60 that we know of gave their lives to Christ in three evenings. The local co-ordinator said that in Spain a quarter of that number would have been a miracle.

Then in Bielefeld, some 20 or so churches and about 200 team members went out onto the streets together and, in that reserved country, found a wonderful welcome (perhaps the fantastic sausages – *Bratwurst* – had something to

do with it!) and a full-time German On the Move organisation came into being. We felt the Lord doing immensely
deep things in twinning the church in Germany with the
church in England, together able to take the gospel to the
world. If that kind of reconciliation between two previously
warring nations could be seen in action, how much more
could others be led into reconciliation?

From then on it was clear, both to ourselves and to our
German counterparts, Heinrich and Sabine Baumann, that
Germany was to have a key role in the international vision
for 2005; that it would be something which, in a real way,
the two nations could do together. Germany was 'pregnant'
with a new role in international mission, which it was more
than ready to take on. As for Heinrich and Sabine, the Lord
had recently showed them that Sabine should leave her job
and they should make a room in their house ready to be an
office. They did both. A week later we asked them to form
a German On the Move organisation. The Lord had positioned them to be equipped, ready and available.

While in Bielefeld, Gina phoned home and learnt that
one of the children was not behaving properly. Not for the
first time, Gina – a natural and committed mother – said
that she should be at home with her children, not travelling
around the world with me. Only this time she was
adamant. She had made her decision, she said. This was the
last trip she would come on. But what was the Lord's view
on this? I knew how important Gina was to the operation
of On the Move, not just in terms of giving me personal support and encouragement, but also in terms of making relationships everywhere we went, hearing sometimes very
precisely from God and having a spiritual authority that

sometimes alone did the trick. I could not imagine doing this without her.

In the event, the Lord himself stepped in. A member of the German team in Bielefeld approached Gina the very next day and said that she had a 'word' for her. A time was arranged for them to meet up. The lady proceeded to tell her, 'The Lord is saying to you, Gina, where your husband goes, you go. Do you understand?' she asked insistently. She repeated the statement twice more, just to make sure.

*   *   *

At this point, the Lord started putting together the new team ahead of the 2005 missions. Peter, a member of our church home group, became our administrator. David and Barbara, with us in Nigeria, joined to travel with us as we took the vision around the world.

In September of that year, I fell ill and – for the first time ever – was too ill, apparently with some sort of virus, to attend a mission I was supposed to lead in Bognor Regis on the south coast of England. What should we do? My eldest daughter Cristina and her husband Nick had been around OTM for years. Nick had led worship at so many missions, and both of them had become our best recruiters – that is to say, people who would do presentations in half a dozen churches on a Sunday morning to present the vision of a forthcoming mission and recruit the team. They were excellent at it, clearly anointed and full of energy. On the spur of the moment, with me out of action for Bognor, we decided to ask them to lead the mission – with Gina being there in the background to give support if necessary – and see how they did.

They did brilliantly. We had loads of comments about how anointed they were, how naturally they fitted into the role ('as to the manor born', 'chip off the old block', etc.) and how wonderful it was to see the new generation spreading its wings in leadership. Kerry, our chairman, said that it was frequently the case in the kingdom of God that children inherited an anointing and a calling from their parents; that if they were clearly gifted, then this was very good news indeed and we should employ them to take on the UK missions. The other trustees were wholly supportive of the idea – as were Nick and Cristina when we told them. It turned out that they had dreamed of being able to do this, but hadn't dared to ask.

Part 3

9

Airborne

If you have a vision to do missions in the 30 main capital cities of the world, and you are running a not-very-significant evangelistic organisation in the UK, how do you go about seeking to fulfil this calling? A couple of factors need to be borne in mind. First, we had no international network to call on (some organisations do; we didn't; we were starting from scratch, without contacts). Second, we had no money. On the Move had grown over five or six years into an organisation that could just about support itself in its ministry through an accustomed round of missions, which gave rise to a flow of donations, which was always enough to pay the salaries. Although it remained a faith venture, there was a pattern about missions and donations, and a backlist of supporters who gave by monthly banker's order, which made OTM likely to 'wash its face'. But now the rules were changing. We were to rely on the same funding base as ever, yet henceforth we were to do UK missions, pay UK mission salaries *and* undertake repeated and extremely expensive international journeys and employ staff who would mainly operate internationally, all from the same minor pot of resources. Impossible! So we were now thrown into a new venture of faith, just as we might have been inclined to get comfortable in continuing the old one.

So we had no contacts, no money (literally none, to make *any* of these trips) and no obvious route towards making this huge mission a goer. And, of course, a mission linking the world's major capitals had never been done. It was a 'stretch target' in so many respects. How might we at least start the process?

I had a 'quiet day' with the Lord – I think my second ever. At the first, about six months before, I had received (almost like a dictation) a brand-new training evening plan for OTM missions, all based on selected passages in Isaiah (chapters 52–61), which seemed to capture with a new depth the heart of what the Lord was doing. Now, the Lord gave me the bones of a strategy. These were the results:

- We made a video, showing 15 minutes of footage from missions in five countries (Germany, Spain, UK, France and Nigeria) – the basis of our presentations abroad.
- We knew it was now right to speak openly of the vision for 2005. We mailed 14,000 former team members with a brochure that said what we felt called to do, asking for financial and prayer support and participation in travelling teams.
- We created a logo – Gina had seen this in her mind and then painted it. It was the flags of the 30 nations we were to approach, lined up as if on a scarf, which was draped over the cross, hanging down on both sides. It was a wonderful image of unity between nations, based on the cross.

- We started to think and work towards the goal of visiting all 30 capitals to present the vision.

Sending the mailing to all our team members was itself a leap of faith. There was nothing there yet to validate what we were doing; and yet I knew God was saying that we had to put our faith on the line and declare the vision boldly, whether people would take it seriously or not. God was not allowing us to exercise normal caution in only declaring the vision when it was already being fulfilled. We had to go for it now and accept that there would be egg all over our faces if it didn't turn out as we hoped.

The first presentation we did was in Madrid, in tandem with preparations for the Mostoles mission (Mostoles being a big town on the edge of Madrid). Our contact there, Jaime Villareal, was not only the pastor of a church in Mostoles but was also one of the co-ordinators of the Madrid churches. He invited us to do a presentation to the pastors of about 40 churches in and around the capital, and I told them about the vision for 2005. They welcomed it, they loved it, and Jaime ('Jimmy') took it upon himself to organise it. By the time we arrived to do the Mostoles mission, Jimmy had already spent a week with us in the UK during the final week of the north of England mission – and had toured with us, seeing no less than seven towns in mission that week. So convinced was he that this was of God, that he didn't baulk when he failed to get official permission for the Mostoles mission, but opted to do it anyway (and in the event without incident).

*   *   *

By October 2003 we were off on our first big trip, to South
Africa and then Kenya, organised by a Kenyan clergyman
who had participated in the Newcastle mission in 2000. In
South Africa we spoke to a group of about 60 leaders, who
loved the vision – and they were actually pleased to be
asked 'at last' to pay for their own mission. (We ourselves
would come for free, as usual, but the food had to be their
gift to their people.) Time and time again, this twin-track
approach to the funding of missions simultaneously moved
people and challenged them. This is remarkable, because
the lack of a financial carrot – indeed, a requirement instead
that they should *spend* money – should by rights have made
an already impossible vision all the harder to fulfil.

As we arrived in South Africa, Gina had a picture of
hands – black, white and Asian – placed together between
the hands of Jesus. We knew that unity between the races
would be the key. Meanwhile, I had the word 'fault-lines'
in my mind. I felt the Lord was saying that, in the racial
divides in South Africa, there were fault-lines which
extended to much of the earth, but which had their epicen-
tre, as it were, in South Africa – once the world's most notorious example of institutionalised racism. When this
stronghold was broken, I believe the Lord said, the spiritual
impact would be worldwide and one of Satan's most successful strategies would be countered. And only the church
could do it, by walking in unity. The black and white leaders we met were very taken with this vision and agreed that
they must work together in joint teams, seeking also to
bring in the 'coloureds' (as they call them there) and Asians.

The Lord, however, was taking this further. We were taken to meet the head of the churches' economic transformation think tank. We didn't quite know why we were there, and nor did Dr Mongezi Guma, who welcomed us. But as we spoke, Dr Guma said that he had been asking the Lord why we were there and felt that our coming was significant. Could he tell us the story of Sophiatown?

It emerged that Sophiatown had been a black town of about 60,000 people where, on the 9th February 1955, in one of apartheid's most notorious acts, the bulldozers had moved in and flattened the town – all except the Anglican church – in order to move out the black population and make of Sophiatown a new, whites-only town. Dr Guma was now vicar of the Anglican church there. Amongst the white population of Sophiatown, there was not a little guilt at how they had come to be there. There was also fear – to the extent that when, every 9th February, many displaced black people tended to come back to seek their roots, some of the whites had in the past stoned them. But the focus of this annual pilgrimage was the Anglican church, the only building surviving from the old days. Dr Guma felt that the church occupied a unique position for both communities. Could an On the Move mission, bringing together the races, be the vehicle God was wanting to use to bring reconciliation?

We sat there around this boardroom table, deeply moved by what we were hearing and sensing a call from God. There were seven of us from OTM, including Heinrich and Sabine from Germany, and it was Heinrich who pointed out something of key importance. The previous day we had arranged a mission in Pretoria for the second week of

February, 2005. That week just happened to include the 9th February, which in this case would, by some extraordinary coincidence, be the exact fiftieth anniversary of the bull-dozers arriving at Sophiatown. And we had *already* arranged to come then! We were all quite awestruck at what God seemed to be putting together here. It was agreed that we would come, with a team, and look to do missions in both Sophiatown (8th–9th February) and Pretoria (10th–12th February). Dr Guma would consult other churches in Sophiatown and we would be in touch about it.

Just a rider about Sophiatown. Gina was in a bookshop some months later when she felt the Holy Spirit say, 'Buy that book.' It was Nelson Mandela's *Long Road to Freedom*. Gina thought there might be something about Sophiatown, but then again, it did cost £20. She wasn't sure, and left it. Days later, we visited a dear friend suffering from Parkinson's disease. Gina said to me, 'Tell him about Sophiatown.' This is strange, I thought. His concentration rarely lasts for more than half a sentence and the story of Sophiatown is a complex issue to put across to someone in that condition. But I took Gina's prompt and started to tell our friend about the town. He heard me out and then said, 'Oh yes, I know all about Sophiatown: it's where Trevor Huddleston used to campaign against the proposed demolition – there's a lot about it in Nelson Mandela's book, which is over there.' It emerged that a young woman had been coming in once a week to read to him from this book. She often wondered whether he was taking anything in. Now it was clear that he had taken it all in! We borrowed the book, which had about eight pages on the struggle to save Sophiatown in 1955. I later told Dr Guma about our experience with this book. He was most moved and resolved all the more to pull a mission together.

In Kenya, about 50 gathered for a breakfast meeting. Before I had a chance to do my presentation, Gina said she had something to say. As she spoke to the group, she was in floods of tears and said that her heart was breaking with what the Lord was showing her: there was no unity; each person was coming with their own agenda, pursuing their own interests – and they didn't even have a heart for the person sitting next to them.

Now, this approach would *not* make it into a volume of *How to Make Friends and Influence People*. It is not an easy thing to speak a word of rebuke to the very people one wishes to persuade to do an On the Move mission! And yet, the impact of what she said was profound. A spirit of repentance came upon the meeting. All agreed that God had spoken. All agreed that the mission would be a wonderful way to pursue the unity they knew they lacked. We made dates for mid-February 2005, just after the missions in South Africa.

We took a break for a day and a half, visiting the Masai Mara game reserve – an amazing experience. On the way back we stopped at a roadside shop. A number of young men were loitering outside, apparently with nothing to do. One talked to Gina, who said she was from England. He asked for her leftover foreign change and she explained that we weren't rich – we were missionaries who were living by faith. She asked what he did, and he said he wanted to move to Nairobi to look for work. Gina said that there was a lot of unemployment there and that maybe he should finish his education and use his skills (she sensed that he was a natural leader) to help make something of the community where he lived. Would he like her to pray for him?

'Wait a moment,' he said. He came back with several other men, who all lined up to receive prayer. Within a couple of minutes there were no fewer than 25 of them. The six of us spread out to pray for each one individually – a moving experience as we saw one after the other touched by the Holy Spirit. I then introduced David, saying that he would love to explain to them how they could ask Jesus into their lives. This David did, and all 25 received Jesus. The last one to arrive had been the chief of the tribe, and he too gave his life to Christ and we had the privilege of praying for him. The most touching thing for me was to see the difference between the sullen faces when we arrived, and the radiant faces as we left.

We sometimes pray for these people still – and were later to see them again. On that occasion, 18 months later, the joy on the face of Joseph, the chief, was priceless. 'I really never thought I would see you again – this is so wonderful!' he said. It was good for our souls, too!

*   *   *

Our first trip – our first 'missionary journey', as it were – was completed. We had seen God take over and impose his agenda in each country in a remarkable way. There was no predicting what the Lord would do. We just had to be obedient and go with the flow. There was no question that God was with us and was placing his seal on the project in a very tangible way as we travelled to communicate the vision. It was also clear that the Missions 2005 vision was already touching deep veins of both history and the contemporary life of the church.

*   *   *

Over the next couple of months, subsequent trips were organised. There were three regional trips, each incorporating three capitals, organised for the end of January 2004 through to the end of March. How did we make the contacts? To give you the flavour of how God was working this one out, here are some examples.

Seoul. A vicar in East Birmingham phoned us to say he was receiving visitors from Seoul. Would we like to meet them? They came for lunch. The leader of the Korea All Nations Mission loved the vision. Gina had a prophetic word for him, which impacted him greatly. Then she said she felt the Lord saying that when we came to South Korea, we should bring a team of 'emerging young leaders', who would be a blessing to the Korean church. He was now in tears: it turned out that the Lord had commissioned him to link emerging young leaders from the UK with emerging young leaders from South Korea. The Korean church, a very strong church, was weak when it came to reaching the young.

Cairo. A pastor of a big church in Cairo was ministering in Lyon, France, at the time of our mission there. He loved what he saw and said, 'Come!'

Ottawa. Jeffrey Brandt, our former administrator during Missions 2000, is Canadian. Of all places, he had now settled in the smallish city of Ottawa, the Canadian capital. He had said to me, 'If you ever want me to organise a presentation with Ottawa pastors, just let me know.'

Mexico City. Jimmy from Spain made contact for us with the president of the Evangelical Fellowship of Mexico, who invited us to come.

Japan. A contact there decided to check us out by writing to someone he happened to know in Birmingham, to ask if he was aware of On the Move and could vouch for us. Who did he write to? The leader of Gina's and my house group (membership: twelve people)!

By the end of January, everything was in place and the tickets were bought. There was just one thing. Two days before making the first of these trips, I learnt that I had cancer.

10

Shadow of the Valley

The opening chapter of this book was written on the 29th January 2004, on the plane to Tokyo – the first of these trips. You may remember that I had seen a tumour in my mouth while I was looking in the car mirror. Two days later I had an emergency operation. Seven days after that (two days before the Tokyo trip) we were told the results of the biopsy: it was cancer, and quite a virulent form at that.

Basically, I would need a very large operation to get rid of the remaining cancer. The consultant promised to try and work around my travel dates. And so it was that, the day I wrote the first chapter, I was indeed on a plane – weak from the operation, but getting better.

What was going on? It seemed clear to us that this was an attack from Satan. Our best guess, and that of others whose wisdom and discernment we trusted, was that Satan was trying to render the whole programme for 2005 stillborn. Which made me all the more determined that we were *not* going to give him satisfaction. Somehow, I knew that the missions *would* happen. I knew that the Lord was not going to allow this vision to be derailed. I wasn't so sure what was going to happen to me, except that I had received the word from the Lord that 'you are not going to die'. It was an extraordinary situation to be in, to be flying out to share the vision of missions in 30 capital cities for 2005, not actually knowing if I would still be alive by then, except for my inner conviction that the word I felt the Lord had given me was truly from him.

The statistics were not good. It later emerged that 60 per cent of people with this kind of cancer die from it. The other 40 per cent can't speak properly. The speech therapist said to me, 'I'm very concerned about the idea that you want to continue doing public speaking.' The operation would make this impossible – 'this' being my whole ministry. If that wasn't bad enough, the radiotherapy I would subsequently have to submit to would kill all my salivary glands, giving me a permanently dry mouth. And, just for good measure, my taste buds would be killed too, making all food taste like cardboard from then on.

It was with this background, facing a very major operation some time in the next two months and radiotherapy thereafter, that we embarked on our tour of the Far East, the Middle East and North America (or at least as much of it as we would be able to do before the operation of unknown date), to present the vision of what we were supposedly to come back and do with them the following year. All we had was God's word that I was not going to die, and a sense (no – a clear knowledge) that he was with us, and that the vision for 2005 was from him.

This was weakness – and if God's strength is truly 'made perfect in weakness', we could look forward to a high degree of perfection! But, seriously, On the Move had always been predicated on weakness. In this, there was nothing new. We had also seen some spectacular rescues in our time and had sound reason to hope and even expect that God would pull something out of the bag this time. There was also an inner conviction that we needed to press forward and continue what we had started. This didn't mean that I wasn't going to feel trepidation. But I was (and we were) to go on regardless. That was vital.

*   *   *

In terms of my immediate physical condition following the first operation, I was weak and had experienced a fair bit of pain, especially when trying to eat even liquidised food. There was, after all, a gaping hole in the roof of my mouth. Gina brought a carrier bag full of jars of baby food for me to eat on the journey. But somehow I sensed that I only needed to take the step of getting onto the plane and things would immediately improve. And it was so. It was on the flight to Japan that I was able to have my first solid food. I knew I was being prayed for by many. Our prayer emails had gone out to hundreds and we had received an astounding number of moving replies, cards, and so on. Now it felt good just being on the job.

Actually, being abroad was itself a great tonic. We could leave our children secure, as Nick and Cristina had dropped everything (the very day Gina cried out to the Lord for a solution) to come down from the Lake District and hold the fort. We were so grateful for this, as for other acts of kindness, not least from our church in Harborne. The challenge now was to present a vision dear to my heart to the church in Tokyo – and I was up for that challenge! Many times, during the next ten days in the Far East, I completely forgot about my condition, heartened by what the Lord was doing in our midst.

Tokyo was a lovely experience. Our host Wolfgang, the Overseas Missionary Fellowship (OMF) director in Japan, was so caring and loving towards us. Gina's baby food jars were never needed and got donated to a missionary couple in Tokyo, who had a real baby! The presentation was inconclusive, however, with plenty of enthusiasm (and wonderful worship, as we sang in Japanese), but with too few Japanese church leaders represented to make a mission definite.

If you've ever worried about a lack of space, you should try the great cities of the Far East. In Tokyo there is low car ownership, not least because there is nowhere near most people's houses to park (but the trains are excellent). In Seoul, our next stop, the tower blocks are built so close together that you could almost reach out from one window and touch the neighbour's window opposite. We are fortunate in so many ways in the West.

What Seoul does have, unlike Tokyo, is a very strong Christian presence. It is moving at night to look at the skyline and see the dozens of identical red neon crosses, each one marking the presence of a church in this once-Buddhist nation. Christianity is now unmistakeably the dominant faith and it was immediately clear that the atmosphere (you could feel it) was so much lighter than that in Tokyo. There is a sense of spiritual freedom in the air in South Korea which is deeply refreshing. We could see the difference manifested in many forms. Whereas in Japan there is silence on the train, even amongst groups of school children (very odd), in South Korea there is a playfulness and lightness amongst the young people that was such a relief to see again.

Religion forms a society. Some societies are free, others desperately bound – I mean spiritually. Again, we take the relative freedom we have in the West for granted. When you visit a country without a Christian heritage, you immediately notice the difference. We don't value enough the spiritual bequest our Christian forefathers gave us. It's still in the air, even if the spiritual equivalent of global warming is threatening and gradually eroding that spiritual 'environment' we inherited.

In Seoul we had lovely meetings with the OMF director and then with the president of the Korea All Nations Mission, with whom we had connected so wonderfully in Birmingham. The latter and, separately, another pastor prayed for my healing, with a love and a passion that I have rarely encountered. I felt waves of the Holy Spirit coming over me – but it was a general experience, and not apparently centred on that specific part of my body that needed repairing. Had God healed me? It was difficult to say.

One rider about Seoul. We were royally hosted by our contacts. The food was amazing (dozens of dishes being brought for each course). And we were never allowed to spend a penny! (English readers shouldn't worry – I mean this literally, not metaphorically. . .)

On to China – another bound country. But there was a tremendous sense of spiritual hunger amongst people we met, and a singular welcome towards people from abroad.

We imagined that a mission would go wonderfully here. We worshipped with one family in their flat on the four-teenth floor of a tower block, a most moving experience. It is this family worship at eight o'clock every evening, and not church services, that we were told was the principal building block of Christian life there. Then we met with eight elders of the (underground) church and they wel-comed the vision, without being clear how we might get permission from the authorities to do something like that in Beijing. We ministered to them all that evening and Gina and Barbara were given personal prophetic words for each of them – and we found ourselves in an almost apostolic role. It was an amazing evening of encouragement and tears, envisioning and strengthening; and one of them prayed for my healing with very great passion. Again, how-ever, it was inconclusive as far as the mission was con-cerned.

We headed back to England. On arrival, I had a rude awakening. Oh. Here we are. I have cancer. It's not over. I still have to face the music.

*   *   *

Actually, the consultant gave us some good news – not about my cancer, but about our travel hopes. We *would* be able to go both to the Middle East and to North America, all four of us. We were due back on the 18th March from the final trip. He would admit me into hospital on the 21st and operate on the 22nd, and my pre-op session would be fitted in during the five days between the two last trips. Now that's what I call a National Health Service!

In the car, on the way back from Heathrow airport following the Japan/Korea/China trip, I hit a low. But after a while, on that car journey, we felt that the Lord wanted to speak to us. Gina gave a message in tongues and I had an interpretation. I believe God said, 'I will sovereignly restore your mouth.' We both received this as from the Lord. This did seem to imply that I would have the operation, as it was the operation (rather than the cancer *per se*) that would damage my mouth. But my voice would be restored.

Yet the stuffing of this renewed faith was once again knocked out of us a few days later when the speech therapist explained to us what we could expect. It was then that she expressed her doubts about my public speaking, adding – as an example – that I might try to make the sound 'pop' and it would come out 'mom'. I just wouldn't be able to pronounce many ordinary words. For Gina and myself that was the low point, notwithstanding what we felt the Lord had said. We both sank, for several days, quite unable to lift ourselves. It was only a visit from our old friend Louise that lifted us. She had specifically heard God tell her to drop everything and visit us – after a gap of more than a year of not being closely in touch. As she prayed for us, our spirits rose and we felt something lift off us.

Soon enough we were off again, to Cairo, Jerusalem and Tel Aviv and then Istanbul. In Cairo, our first Islamic country, the church of about 400 people at which we were based was vibrant and encouraging. The worship was terrific (and very distinctively Arabic – which didn't stop me picking up an electric guitar and jamming with the locals after the service, much to our mutual enjoyment). But the breakthrough came when we got to know Amgad, a Christian businessman. He was at first quite sceptical about the vision we were bringing, not least because he could not imagine local pastors wanting to pay for the food to be given out. But when he challenged us one evening, we talked and talked – and it was one of those occasions when I found the Lord speaking through me, to his heart, and he was captured for the vision in a way that was destined to last. It was he who organised other businessmen to pay for the food (because as a matter of principle we were insisting that we would not do so), and it was he who arranged churches to host missions there. Provisional dates were made and Amgad became a friend. Our evening cruise down the Nile will not be forgotten. And in Cairo, at a large church meeting, the whole congregation prayed for my healing.

Israel was difficult. Our presentation fell through, as the person organising it changed his mind at the last minute. We made a few good contacts, but nothing conclusive. I was prayed for yet again, for healing, in a Tel Aviv church, and I was impacted yet again. We also got to spend a day by the Sea of Galilee, which was a most special time. Yet the going was not proving easy. More cities were saying 'maybe' than 'yes'. In Istanbul, where we met with nine delightful pastors (very much a quorum in a city with a small, persecuted church), the result was another 'maybe'.

*　　*　　*

Back in England again, I had another downer on arrival, although not as severe as the first one. I had my pre-op examination and we then prepared to go on to North America. Our children continued to be incredibly brave. They stayed with dear friends from our church while we were away (one of those friendships where every child is best friends with his or her opposite number, and we with the parents), and we went off for the third and last trip of the series.

Our former administrator, Jeffrey, had sorted things out in Ottawa and, true to his word, had gathered the key leaders. The presentation was ever so well received (I could by now talk totally normally, having recovered fully from the first operation), and we set dates for a mission – and had some spectacularly good meals to boot! It was great to be with old friends and I was most amused to hear Jeffrey saying, 'I think we'll use the Orpington model' (Orpington being an area of London that organised itself for the mission in a way we later copied). This was the house jargon that only a former On the Move administrator could have used – and yet it was now to be put to good use in Canada's capital city!

Then we moved on to Washington DC. First we did a presentation to the Hispanic churches forum, with about 25 pastors present, and then we met key black leaders, who loved the vision too and agreed to take it on. A couple of white churches were initially involved as well, as a sort of 'down payment' on the future. All felt the call to work together. Dates were made for a mission immediately preceding the one in Ottawa (continuing a trend where dates that were right for one county turned out also to be suitable for the next in the same region, enabling us to organise sensible tours; it could so easily have been otherwise). At the second presentation, an evangelist felt moved to come and pray for me for healing. Once again, the Holy Spirit touched me strongly – yet, as ever, not specifically in the area of the mouth.

Finally, we arrived in Mexico. We felt we faced opposition there from the beginning. David was very ill and unable to leave his hotel bedroom – very much unlike him. We prayed, and he got better gradually. Then we started to explore the city. Standing on a high balcony, I had a strangely powerful urge to throw myself off it, to my death. Again we prayed. In the night David, Barbara and I all had nightmares. Also, all arrangements for our presentation there were repeatedly kiboshed. First the national conference at which we were invited to speak got moved to a later date, for domestic reasons. We had to delay our flight home by a day, at significant expense, to accommodate this change. Then the first evening meeting of the conference (which we were to address on the eve of our newly arranged departure) got cancelled too. Finally we visited the main cathedral – not a place we felt at home in, a cold and forbidding place. We prayed there, and took authority over the spiritual forces that we felt were opposing us.

The atmosphere changed immediately. The Lord spoke to us about how his grace was going to flow like a river, how the people would enjoy it like children splashing in a fountain. Then the president of the Mexico evangelical *fraternidad*, who was still trying to do something for us, said he would organise a special meeting in Mexico City for maybe 30 pastors. We thanked him, not quite believing that he would get that many at such short notice. Nor, I think, did he quite believe it either – for no-one was as amazed as he when 140 pastors turned up. They received the vision wonderfully and invited us to return in 2005.

We now had eight cities committed to doing the mission, and there were another five thinking about it. Quite some progress had been made before an enforced pause.

11

Grounded

We got back, a day later than planned, on the 19th March – and I went into hospital on the 21st. Now that it was so near I actually felt more peaceful about it all, and grateful for the distractions that I had enjoyed over the previous two months.

My father, a retired doctor, who had been deeply worried about my condition, came up to spend the first week of my hospitalisation with the family. His presence was enormously helpful and comforting.

He was already himself impacted by what he had seen God do – despite being more or less an atheist. But, as a doctor, he was obviously knowledgeable about what one could and could not expect of the NHS. He said to us around this time that he had been struck by several factors in my case, in particular:

- how I had seen the tumour in the first place, in the car mirror with the sun streaming into my mouth – a highly unusual set of circumstances;

- how the GP had seen me the next day and then got me in to see the specialist the day after that;
- how the surgeon had also been available to see me immediately at the hospital and how it turned out that, due to a cancellation, he was able to operate on me that very day; and how he got me an MRI scan (usual waiting time 15 months) the following day;
- how it just so happened that we live literally five minutes' walk from perhaps Britain's leading centre for precisely this kind of cancer;
- how the NHS had timed everything perfectly to fit our travel dates.

He said he had done a lot of thinking; and he had concluded that he could come up with no other explanation for what he had seen happening other than what I would say, which was that it was the result of so many people praying for me.

There was one further thing that impressed him. As he and Gina walked beside me while I was wheeled through endless corridors towards the operating theatre on the day itself, he saw that I was completely peaceful. And indeed I was. I find that amazing, too!

The operation itself lasted eight hours and apparently a total of about 20 doctors, nurses, anaesthetists and others worked on me during that time. It involved a thick skin graft from my arm, with blood vessels attached, being linked through amazing microsurgery to the blood vessels of my neck, and being used as a sort of patch ('flap', they called it) to replace the part of my hard palate that had been removed. I am tall (six foot three), and I later calculated that the total length of scars (around my palate, neck, arm and abdomen) in aggregate came to more than half my height! When I came round, apparently I looked quite extraordinary ('like Frankenstein'), with one side of my neck twice as thick as the other, and tubes coming to and from every possible angle. When young Nicholas saw me on the second day, he went white and very nearly fainted. This was a hard time for Gina too. She bore it bravely.

Nonetheless, I recovered quickly. On about the third or fourth day, one of the doctors said that in about 150 cases of this kind of surgery, he had *never* seen anyone recover that quickly. Soon I was up and about, and writing voluminous notes to everyone. I couldn't speak at that point.

After ten days, I left hospital. Already my voice (though clearly impaired by the operation – I couldn't pronounce all sorts of sounds) was said to be 'remarkable'. Perhaps most remarkable of all was the fact that, although I experienced real discomfort, I actually experienced no *pain* at all – and that freedom from pain lasted.

We had a week in Wales and a wonderful family time. Four weeks after the operation, we went to see the two surgeons to find out what had been shown up by the analysis of what they had removed. Their technique was to 'section' it, so that they would know exactly where the cancer was in relation to what had been removed and, consequently, whether enough clearance around the edge of it had been achieved to make the operation a success. On that depended the extent of radiotherapy that I would need.

It was really the radiotherapy that I feared the most. I really, really didn't want to lose my salivary glands and my taste buds. Moreover, I had recovered so well from the operation: having to go through radiotherapy would be like just managing to crawl out of a deep hole, only to be kicked back down into it again.

Well, Gina and I arrived to meet my two surgeons – and they were both grinning like Cheshire cats. They said they had analysed the results and, to their amazement, *no trace of cancer had been found*. Because of this, no radiotherapy would in fact be needed, as there was absolutely nothing there to treat. This was a remarkable miracle, as the cancer had clearly been there before our foreign trips – before I had received so much prayer for healing. Waves of relief came over us both. And then joy. What a moment!

In the final part of our interview with the surgeons, they told us that we would need to come in every couple of weeks at first, and then just occasionally for check-ups. This, one of them said, was not so much because there was anything wrong with me, but because, with the mortality rate running at 60 per cent and real problems remaining for the other 40 per cent, it was so *encouraging* to the staff to see someone like me!

The three-month convalescence was a real bonus. It gave us some much needed family time. It gave us a break from incessant travelling and exertion over six years of being 'on the move'. It gave me a chance to catch my breath, to think, to read. It gave Gina and myself an opportunity to recharge our batteries. It gave the contacts we had been making around the world time to gestate, without pressure.

More good came out of it. We had held that fundraising dinner in London the night before flying off to Tokyo, where people had been moved. While in Japan, I received a text message from my daughter Natalia, saying that some-one there had sent in a cheque for £15,000. Others also gave generously, and so did people who just heard what we were going through. One of the miracles of this campaign around the world was always going to be that God supplied the money for our team to visit 30 countries – twice!

We received so much support and so much love. I think the cancer had an important part to play in galvanising the support, of all kinds, that we were to receive from so many.

Above and beyond all this, my relationship with my father has been transformed, as has my relationship with my sister, Nina.

As for the work itself, when we started travelling again to Paris and Brussels after the three months were over – and I found that my voice was already very nearly restored (a key, and in a sense quite separate, miracle) – it became clear that church leaders were stirred by this testimony and felt confirmed in their sense that this was from God, that Satan had tried to destroy it, and that they would all the more embrace it as a result. Thus something that was sent to derail what God was doing was now serving to expedite it.

*   *   *

Since that time, my voice has returned to normal. It is not just that I can pronounce anything, as normal. It is also that the timbre of my voice is now apparently unchanged from what it used to be. I have as much power in my voice as I ever had. All in all, God performed a remarkable miracle for me and we are all so very grateful. My surgeon, who averages about 100 of these operations per annum, said recently, 'Your recovery is absolutely amazing. To tell you the truth, I have never seen anyone recover so completely from this kind of surgery.'

I sometimes get reminders of what we went through. But now, as I write this part of the book in November 2004, just over seven months after the operation – on my way to the thirteenth country, in the fifth continent, in the last two months – I can really say that it is all just a memory. God did it, fully. My energy levels are as good as anyone else's in the team. My testimony still stirs hearts all over the world. 'It is wonderful in our eyes', and we continually thank God for his goodness.

12

A Look Back

It is far from easy to describe the experience of going through something as fundamental as facing cancer – facing, indeed, the real possibility of death, the likely end to my ministry, not to mention the prospect of awkward speech, a permanently dry mouth, no taste buds and so on. You will understand that the process was a difficult one. The same could surely be said for the process of carrying a dream for what is to happen in the following year around the world and seeing the whole thing apparently hanging over a precipice. How to cope?

I remember, for example, facing up to the following question: since I am told that I won't be able to do public speaking ever again, should I – while I can – have myself videoed delivering a typical training evening for On the Move? At least then it would be there to be shown to people if and when I became unable to deliver it in person. I knew, however, that the Lord was restraining me from this option. What I mean is that I felt my spirit recoil at the idea, rather than rise to it. I also had the word which I believed to be from God that he would 'sovereignly restore' my mouth. What I'm saying here is not so much that I had faith (I did, but that isn't everything) – more that I was broadly at peace about it all and ready to follow the sense I had in my heart that the answer to this idea was a 'no'.

How could I be at peace? Notwithstanding the relief we both strongly felt when we received the 'all clear', it remains the case that we had been broadly peaceful *most* of the time when things remained unclear. How could this be? How could I be at peace even while being wheeled towards the operating theatre for a massive operation? Is it that I'm somehow just wired that way? Didn't I feel the emotions that others would feel? Is such peace (or faith) possible?

I want to say that this has been more an attitude of heart than a state of mind; and that, in addition to a gift of peace given at the moment it was most needed, this attitude of heart has also in fact been the long-term fruit of a long-term journey – a process through which God has put me.

I also want to say that I was not always like this.

Here is a glance at my background, my conversion to Christianity and the early journey on which the Lord took me – and ultimately both Gina and me. These were the times which built the foundations for what has happened since.

*   *   *

I grew up in a well-to-do and (from a refugee point of view) 'assimilated' household, apparently far removed from any memories of its turbulent background – a household which came to seem and feel much like any other middle-class English family. I went to a public (fee-paying) school and grew up speaking 'BBC English' (mainly because my father had been taught his own English by a thoroughly upper-class family in London just before the war).

Nonetheless, there was an insecurity in me that I guess mirrored the insecurity of my parents' experience, and in particular my mother's volatile, if brilliant and lively, character. My father was a much steadier presence, although he would probably agree that he repressed, rather than expressed, his feelings. Meanwhile, a close friend of my parents nicknamed 'Mamie', who became a sort of second mother to my sister Nina and myself (while living a few hundred metres away), was a wonderful peacemaker in an otherwise over-intense family.

I was not, it has to be said, good at school. For a start, I tended to be picked on by others, at least until I was about 16 and found myself a whole lot taller than most – after which I was left alone. Academically I was slow and something of a dreamer. When interviewed for my school at the age of eight, I was asked a simple question about a mathematical problem and spent an inordinate amount of time mulling it over. The headmaster asked me how I was getting on (someone had to say something!) and apparently I replied, 'I'm getting on fine, Sir. I'm just being a little bit slow.' He (a Christian, it seems, who later went into the ministry) seems to have been charmed by this and I was offered a place.

At any rate, I struggled on academically and would have done worse had it not been for Mamie's help and encouragement. I barely scraped through my O levels at the age of 16, and the year before my A levels (due to be taken at 18) I *failed* two out of three subjects and achieved a narrow pass in the third. No-one expected me to go to university – and this in a school where progression to Oxford or Cambridge was almost routine.

Then, at the age of 17, I miraculously got interested! It happened suddenly and in the nick of time, with about eight months to go before my A level exams. I started to find history enjoyable and took notes from my textbook without being forced to. French literature became something I could comment on with interest and I even managed to speak a bit of the language. Economics and politics were ignited as a lifelong interest.

So it was that I managed to achieve reasonable grades in my A levels – not brilliant, but enough to get to university. Which was just as well, because I wasn't good for anything else, let alone the real world. I successfully applied to Swansea, having loved the campus I saw there by the sea. I had no idea that in Swansea I was to become a Christian.

*   *   *

In Swansea I made a number of friends and, while remaining quite insecure in many ways, I did start to spread my wings. I did increasingly well academically and started to be active in student politics, founding a Liberal Club and putting great energy into it. I was the second president of this club. I also (in year two) found myself next-door neighbours in the hall of residence with the president of the Conservative Club on one side and the vice-president of the Labour Club in the room beyond him – someone's idea of a joke, I think. Next to me on the other side was a Christian.

We all had long conversations into the night, as students do, be it about politics or philosophy – or religion. And, almost whatever it was we were talking about, I found myself inclined to agree with Simon, the Christian in the room next door. Simon wore his tie outside his sweater and did one or two other uncool things besides. But he had a peace and a wisdom (apart from the tie, that is) about him – and I felt safe with him. Perhaps he just showed me love. I also believe I had been in some way prepared for understanding the Christian perspective by avidly reading the C.S. Lewis 'Narnia' books as a child and drawing from these a sense of the way things should be. Something was now striking a deep chord in me.

I didn't give Simon an easy ride. We started to have long discussions about Christianity – the problem of suffering; the difficulty of making 'simplistic' moral choices (for example, if the baddies are chasing someone, do you, when asked, tell them the truth about which way they went for the sake of truthfulness, or do you lie to save the victim? I must have been the evangelist's worst nightmare). This process went on for about four months, with Simon being infinitely patient and sensitive. He also suggested that I read St John's Gospel. I did so and was in fact impressed with what I perceived to be the 'authenticity' of it. I did feel these to be the words of God. But I wasn't particularly animated to do anything about it. Patience really is sometimes needed to let a seed grow in its own time!

Simon then invited me to a university 'mission' (whatever that was), a week-long affair led by a visiting speaker. I wasn't particularly interested and must have disappointed Simon by not making the effort to go all week – until the

Saturday, the last day, on which I suppose I had nothing better to do.

I remember being quite impressed by the shining eyes of the evangelist, Roger Forster. I felt there was a real sincerity there. He did also answer a crucial question for me that night, which was *how to connect* with God. I actually felt there was a wide chasm between God and myself, even though I liked what I was seeing about the Christian faith. How could one cross this gulf? How could I actually reach God? Roger Forster quoted the verse from Revelation 3:20, where Jesus says, 'Here I am! I stand at the door and knock. If anyone hears my voice and opens the door, I will come in and eat with him, and he with me.' A penny really did drop. So it was *God* who was willing to take the initiative in reaching me, rather than *me* having to locate and then reach him. That made it all quite possible and, if so, I was willing.

Forster suggested that we might want to pray a prayer asking Jesus into our life there and then, or else we might choose to do it later back in our room. Being the sort who didn't want to feel that I was doing someone else's bidding, I chose the latter option. That night, I knelt by my bed (as I imagined one was supposed to do) and, as best as I knew how, repented of my sins and asked Jesus to come into my life and be my Lord. That was the 15th February 1975.

*　　*　　*

I told Simon what I had done the next day, and he seemed pleased (if apparently unexcited). He invited me to the Christian Union the next Saturday, and I went. What surprised me most was what happened when I spoke to individuals there and told them my name. The kind of reply I would get was, 'Oh, *you're* Martin!' or words to that effect, which I now realise meant that they had all been praying for me. At the time, I just regarded it as an unexplained curiosity.

I didn't feel ready for church yet. But a fortnight later I announced to Simon that I was happy to go with him. So we walked together the half hour it took to reach the small evangelical Anglican fellowship where Simon went, at the top of a steep hill. Thenceforth, those half-hour walks to church on a Sunday morning were some of my happiest times.

In that first service, it came to Holy Communion. What with my Jewish background, I didn't actually know what to do! So Simon said, 'Follow me and do what I do.' Fair enough, but Simon made up the last in one row kneeling at the altar, and so I had to be the first at the other end. So now what? The pleasant young vicar came with some bread, and that seemed self-explanatory. Then he came with the cup, and I did what any normal person would do. . . I started drinking. And drinking. Then I felt firm hands restraining the cup from sloping any more, and I gracefully let go. I said to Simon later that I thought I had drunk too much, but he assured me that he didn't think God would mind.

Well, I grew as a Christian slowly and certainly undramatically. A nice family at the church befriended me and invited me to the odd Sunday lunch. My views were pretty liberal, and so was much of my conduct. But there was a joy that I began to have and I did feel slightly more secure in myself.

I got my degree (missing, albeit very narrowly, the First I had hoped for). I applied to Cambridge to do research in political philosophy and got rejected. But, just after hearing that, I heard I had won a national essay competition in the field of international relations – the Cecil Peace Prize – and that I was the first undergraduate to win it. Armed with this, I reapplied to Cambridge, this time of course with a topic in the field of political thought about international relations, and was accepted. My dad had to telephone me in the United States to tell me that I'd got in. He was trying to tell me, 'You've been accepted at St John's College, Cambridge!' but the background noise of 500 screaming kids in the American summer camp dining room was such that I kept having to say, 'What?' Finally, I got it!

*   *   *

Where would my faith go from here? Christian-wise, the move to Cambridge was not initially so very good. I decided to go to the college chapel on Sunday mornings and, to be honest, found in retrospect, a year later, that my life had been starved of faith in the way that a man might be starved of food. Only (and unlike food deprivation) I didn't notice a thing at the time. One has to be thankful that God has you in hand even when you manifestly don't have yourself in hand.

My academic supervisor, Professor Sir Harry Hinsley, soon to become master of the college and then vice chancellor of the university, was an absolutely delightful man – a wonderfully English eccentric who always had to drink his tea in his musky book-filled room from his favourite pink mug which was, of course, cracked. He was very kind to me and appreciative of my work. Cambridge was, of course, a wonderful place to be.

But how might God manoeuvre me back to himself? I had in effect drifted right away.

In the April of the first year of my PhD course, Mamie died. This caused great sadness. It also caused me to inherit £9,000, which in those days (1977) was almost enough to buy a terraced house, which I promptly did. Moving to the house in Sturton Street, Cambridge, I decided on the first Sunday to try the local parish church. It was packed. There must have been four or five hundred people there. It was very informal and also surprisingly passionate. I noticed one elderly man praying out loud (this church had an 'open time of prayer', lasting 20 minutes) so passionately that he forgot to pray in English and moved instead into what I assumed must have been his mother tongue.

I had in fact stumbled upon St Matthew's, then Cambridge's main charismatic church – a pioneering example of Anglican charismatic worship, and this 'foreigner' was in fact a local man giving a message in tongues.

Anyway, I loved it. I loved the relaxed nature of it and what I felt to be the genuineness of the experience of God. I joined, and was a 'soft touch' for what came next.

Not many weeks later, I was with an elderly 'elder' of the church who often had students around to his flat. He explained to me about being filled with the Holy Spirit and asked me if I would like him to pray for me to receive this. It sounded like a good idea. I had no preconceptions or baggage to cause me problems in this area and readily accepted being prayed for. When he encouraged me to pray in tongues, I tried to utter a few words and fell about laughing, feeling embarrassed and thinking I was probably making it up. He assured me I wasn't and instructed me to pray in tongues for a while every day.

This was a major turning point. Now I knew joy again – and much more strongly than the first time. I also became infinitely more secure in myself, almost confident, almost overnight. I eagerly lapped up the Scriptures and loved church. I was invited to join a Christian rock band named Fax (I was lead guitarist; *fax* was the Latin for a burning torch and, in 1977, nothing more!). I also became active in helping to run the church youth group and was very committed to this. Indeed, work started to come a poor third.

The honeymoon period was not to last. The peace had overlain the insecurity, rather than eradicating it. It only took a few setbacks, often insignificant in themselves, to rekindle the old sense of vulnerability and a renewed loss of confidence. It was as if the wind simply changed direction, and I was thrown into a lengthy period of self-doubt. I guess God had to deal with the issues of the heart and not allow them to be brushed under the carpet. But that didn't make it fun.

I had long had a tendency towards self-analysis and self-criticism. This was now magnified, in a sense, by my beliefs. I now had a *spiritual* language with which to describe – and add apparent significance to – my self-critical thoughts. Now, simple self-doubt or over-intensity about everything could masquerade as a supposed call to repentance, or to some 'act of faith' or self-denial. I think this is called immaturity. It was certainly hard work. It led me into a quite introverted period of searching, in which I was responding more (I can say in retrospect) to my own insecurities than to the voice of God.

It was Gina who was sent by the Lord to rescue me from this confusion. She nursed me back into something approaching self-confidence. Her love has continued to be a rock for me.

The most important thing, however, was that the two of us resolved together to seek God. We built on our respective foundations of faith in a united quest to see our marriage as one that would have the Lord at the centre. And this has been the real rock that has kept us both through thick and thin.

Looking recently through my 'prophecy file', I was really struck by a word we noted down as being from the Lord back in 1988. It said this:

> I've called you to be my servants, says the Lord. Faithfully serve me and look to do my work. I ask you to give me your full attention; I ask you to be ready to sacrifice yourselves at my altar. I ask you to be ready to die to yourselves so that you might live more fully, more truly in me. I ask you to be mine and fully at my disposal and this is a matter, quite simply, for your decision – whether you are truly to live for me, or whether you'd rather that it is I that serve you. You must choose how you are going to live your lives and you must know the consequences of whichever way you choose and the different paths that are before you now – and I'll be with you always, whichever choice you make.

I find it almost chilling to contemplate the 'wrong' path that we could have chosen. Not that the Lord would have failed to be with us – the word confirms that he would be, in any case. No – it is what we would have missed out on, had we taken the path of least resistance then.

To be sure, the path has been a rocky one since then. We have often wished it would be easier. But we gave permission to the Lord, many years ago, to prune us and hone us and help us to have, and then maintain, a heart after his own heart. This has involved the many ups and downs you have read about in this book – and some more besides. That seems to be how the Lord prunes and hones. But it has also involved ever more precious glimpses of his glory, as we see him act and as all this testing of our faith brings results that could come no other way. It has also involved a growing peace, as 'the worries of this life and the deceitfulness of wealth' (Matthew 13:22) start to take a lower profile, so that the fears, by the same token, come to take on a much less terrible aspect.

Why am I telling you all this? What I want you to understand is that I am an 'ordinary guy' who grew into the things of God in the same way that any other ordinary person can. I was not born peaceful – if anything, I was born nervous! I was not blessed in any special way with a character that would effortlessly lead me into the things of God. On the contrary, left to my own devices, I lurched this way and that and had (have) to deal with any number of aspects to my character of which I am not proud.

Yet I was given glimpses of the things of God – and have made it my aim to seek them out, to believe in what I was glimpsing, and to believe that it was available to me. Persisting in that journey, I found that God himself was putting me through all sorts of experiences and a sort of general purging process that would, over considerable time, bring me to a place where I could go through storms with peace and inner security. I am convinced that this process and this resulting peace is available to all of us, whatever our particular starting point. The Lord longs to be entrusted with each of our particular brands of peccadilloes, sins, insecurities and general no-good characteristics, to bring us from where we are to where we (and he) would like ourselves to be. It is, in fact, his speciality.

It is this honing process which, over years, gradually strips away the things that make for anxiety. In my case, it is the ups and downs I've experienced that have, between them, etched onto my mind lessons that I am not (I hope) about to forget – attitudes of heart that have provided foundations to withstand storms. Here are some things I feel I have come to know *in my heart*. Unless the Lord builds the house, its builders labour in vain (Psalm 127:1) – success is from God. The other pursuits in life that one might have – they are pure vanity (Ecclesiastes 1 – 2); it can all fall apart at the drop of a hat. Don't put your trust in riches, and when they increase, don't set your heart on them (Psalm 62:10). Commit your way to the Lord; trust in him and he will act (Psalm 37:5 RSV). Relax – it'll work out somehow!

That process of pruning and honing which God put us through – that, I would say, has constituted a large part of how we came to be able to survive the 'shaking' of our lives brought about by cancer, the court case, other attacks, the financial crises, and more that was yet to come, in the 'big year' of 2005.

*   *   *

Following three months of convalescence, there were another two months of light work, over July and August. I was able to slip back into work gradually. Somehow, by moving a second Far East trip back from June to September, we managed to schedule visits to all 30 capitals by the end of 2004 as we had planned. That is quite extraordinary, given that visiting so many countries in a year seems impossible enough, without effectively taking five months out in the middle.

What was lost as a result of taking those months out? I did none of the things in respect of the UK missions that I had planned to do that year. But On the Move still managed to field leaders for 19 UK missions that year, thanks in particular to David and Barbara, and also others, who stepped in to lead a number of the missions, and to Nick and Cristina, who did many of the training evenings (to great acclaim) and led several of the missions too. So the cancer served to bring them on. Really, nothing was lost.

It is really the absolute truth to affirm, as Paul does in Romans 8:28, that 'in all things God works for the good of those who love him, who have been called according to his purpose'. Amen and amen.

13

On a Roll

That is almost literally what happened between the 8th September and the 27th November 2004, following the end of my convalescence. In that time we rolled through 14 countries on all five continents – which was going some. Back in June and July, when I was semi-convalescent, we had visited two nearby destinations, Paris and Brussels, with positive responses. Now other doors opened wide. In the Far East, having started with few contacts, our September trip saw us hitting a higher level of church leadership than previously. In Manila, for example, we were received by the director of the Philippines Evangelical Fellowship, who then organised a presentation to local leaders in a key district of the city. In Indonesia, an Islamic country with a large, albeit persecuted, church, we were invited by the Indonesian Evangelical Alliance to address an exclusive meeting of the heads of about a dozen national denominations – who loved the vision, felt sure it was from God and, equally significantly, believed that it would work in their troubled country, and dates were made for a mission.

In fact, having in the earlier part of the year found cities sometimes ready to say an immediate 'yes', but more often wanting to consider the matter further, we now truly found ourselves 'on a roll'. After Singapore, where a 'yes, probably' was tempered by the need to consult others, we had a run of 13 unqualified 'yeses' in a row. Amazing! These (in order) were Manila, Jakarta, Canberra, Wellington, Delhi; then Rome; then Bogotá, Santiago, Buenos Aires, Brasilia and Berlin (all on the same trip); then Abuja in Nigeria, and finally Moscow.

God was granting us real favour. Some places had evidently decided to do the mission before we got there – in Canberra, for example, where we were taken straight from the airport to a barbecue breakfast, set up to give local leaders a flavour of the mission to come! In others, we started from a position of incredible weakness even as we were making the trip. In South America, for example, Jimmy (our dear friend from Spain) had opened up for us key contacts in Colombia and Chile, so that when we got there we were wonderfully looked after by the president of the Bogotá or Santiago pastors' associations. In the latter we spoke to 50 pastors, and in the former to 130 who had gathered specially to hear the vision – and who received it enthusiastically. In Argentina and Brazil, however, it was different. Jimmy had made an arrangement with the key man in Buenos Aires a year before, but in recent months this person had not been returning Jimmy's emails and could not be raised on the telephone. Finally, it was time to make the journey anyway, if only for the sake of other South American cities which *were* expecting us. So we actually arrived at the airport wondering if we would be met and wondering whether anything at all would be in place – and were not too surprised to see that the answer was 'no' and 'no'. We managed to sort ourselves a hotel and a taxi to get us there. We prayed, really very much trusting at this point that the Lord would make a way (he always seemed to). But we didn't have a clue how.

These are the exciting moments – when you see the Lord pluck victory from the jaws of defeat. In this case, Gina phoned Jimmy, who himself made a phone call and then gave us the number of a pastor in Buenos Aires, who he said was now expecting her call. (We would have been able to do *nothing* in Latin America without Gina's Spanish. Everywhere else in the world, English – or occasionally my French – was sufficient; but in Latin America almost no-one we met spoke English. God knew this a long time ago. . .) So Gina phoned this pastor and it turned out that we knew him. We had spent the day with him in Washington DC back in March, when he was there at the same time ministering to the Hispanic churches. He had been to one of our presentations and had loved the vision (and had given me an encouraging word, saying that he was certain I would be healed). Now it turned out that he was the leader of a denomination of 150 churches in Argentina, some 80 of which were in Buenos Aires. He said, 'Leave it to me. . .' (or Spanish words to that effect). Unable to raise the president of the pastors' association (who turned out never to have received the emails), he contacted the vice president and more or less instructed him to pull a meeting together of at least five national denomination heads, for the following morning. In fact six turned up, including the very apologetic president. They loved the vision and we made dates. The next evening another 20 pastors came to hear.

Brazil was no easier. Jimmy had made no headway and there seemed to be a spiritual blockage. About four days before we embarked on the South America trip, we prayed into this and took authority in prayer. Then one of my trustees suggested that I call Ed Silvoso's office in California. They recommended a man who was not in Brasilia itself, but in Sao Paulo. He did have a good network and, being Argentinian, he spoke Spanish as well as Portuguese. Gina emailed him and soon they were speaking on the phone – and he loved the vision. He then said, 'Leave it to me. . .'

When we arrived and met his Brasilia contact, this church leader also liked what he saw of the On the Move vision and then – and only then – decided to invite other pastors to a luncheon the next day, at which I was to present the vision. So, the next morning, with about one or two hours' notice, his secretary began to phone various local pastors, inviting them to lunch at 12.30 p.m., to hear these British missionaries.

It should perhaps be mentioned at this point that people coming from Britain seemed to be quite an event in many of these countries, especially in South America and Asia. In Indonesia and the Philippines, no-one in the respective evangelical alliances could remember receiving a visit from Britain. Likewise in Chile. And yet Britain has a high profile in the Christian field in these countries. Many of them spoke about how they had been influenced by such 'greats' as Whitefield, Wesley, Hudson Taylor, Charles Spurgeon or John Stott. In Colombia and the Philippines, the pastors' association presidents had both been converted through

Englishmen. In Chile, the gospel was first brought to that country by a British missionary. In Korea, the church was started by a Scottish missionary working in China, who began organising for Korean converts there to return and witness in that closed country. In China itself, a senior underground church leader told us with the greatest of pride that he had once met the grandson of Hudson Taylor. This is a digression, but an important one. It seems that there is an expectation in respect of Britain that we have not been fulfilling recently. (This is not for a moment to suggest that there has been no British attention towards those countries – I know people who have served in many of them – but only that it does not have the *profile* it once did.) And an expectation is an opportunity – an open door for ministry.

So it was that, at very short notice and to the amazement of the pastor who had issued the invitations, 25 pastors from Brasilia turned out to hear us. I could immediately see that the ever-so-long table prepared for 30 in the middle of a restaurant was a hopeless situation for a presentation. (My Chamber of Commerce years gave me a strong sense of how to lay out chairs and tables for a meeting!) A quick bit of negotiation led to the other half of the restaurant being opened for us. Apparently, as I went ahead and rapidly moved tables and chairs to create a 'theatre-style' arrangement suitable for a presentation, Brazilian pastors were looking bemused at what this wild Englishman ('he has a wild man anointing!') was doing, single-handedly rearranging the restaurant. Then they twigged what I was up to.

The presentation was wonderfully received. We never got to show the video (except afterwards to a few stragglers) and no pictures could be shown. But they got the vision all right. They were enthusiastic in their response. Dates were arranged for April, and the president of the Brasilia pastors' association said to me in English, 'You can count on me.'

God was doing amazing things on these trips. He would snatch overwhelming victory from seemingly hopeless situations, call together contacts and then meetings out of nothing, somehow communicate across cultures a vision which was translated into the hearts of the hearers as being exactly what they needed. How can the same thing be received in Moscow, Washington DC, Cairo, Santiago, Nairobi and Seoul as exactly what they need to solve their particular problems? Surely, that must be an act of God. As David remarked more than once, 'This is like walking through the book of Acts' – seeing in each country how God did it, watching him pull disparate things together. It was exhausting, but totally exhilarating.

If ever we had doubted the vision, seeing God working in these trips, giving us remarkable favour and organising our every step again and again, certainly convinced us that he was with us all the way, 'with signs following'. Had we come at this project with fame, organisational strength or a network of contacts, we would not have needed these incessant acts of God to make it work. As it was, we did need them and it was a unique experience to walk with the Lord and see him pulling things together apparently out of nothing: very faith-building.

One of the most extraordinary aspects of the thing was how we could (and regularly did) spend two or three days in a country, starting off as total strangers and ending up as true friends – as people with a heartfelt love for and commitment towards one another, and a degree of spiritual bonding that would normally take years, be it in Wellington or Delhi. We would find ourselves ministering to people, encouraging them, receiving highly accurate prophetic words for them and generally being a whole lot more 'fruitful' than we ever were in normal life. People evidently had a sense that what we were carrying was from God. It was deeply attractive to many of them and they found themselves wanting to draw from that well. The Lord truly gave us favour.

Funding kept pace – just. The main donations we received that year were unsolicited. They just came in. I look back in particular at one donation of £5,000, another of £10,000 and one of £15,000, and wonder what would have happened if any one of them had not come.

*   *   *

Abuja, Nigeria, was the twenty-second capital city to say 'yes' to a mission in 2005. This one was helped by glowing reports from the mission in Port Harcourt, and its subsequent impact on the churches that took part.

By the time we got to Moscow, and with only the Netherlands to go (but no invitation yet to visit there), we had a distinct end-of-term feeling. The first night there, just to celebrate and cap an amazing year, we visited the Bolshoi Ballet in their own theatre and, it being nearly Christmas, saw *The Nutcracker*. A more wonderful evening I find it difficult to remember.

Nevertheless, Moscow would surely be a tough nut to crack. It had been difficult to make contacts there and the two people in Moscow to whom I had first talked felt such a mission would not be possible in a city still closely controlled by the authorities and where the evangelical church was used to being blocked at every turn. Yet Gina had a picture from the Lord of a window opening, for just a few years, in which there would be a great opportunity for the gospel in that country, after which things would go bad again. This same word turned out to have been received from at least two other prophets recently. At the meeting we finally had with about a dozen leaders, they welcomed the vision without question, as did one of the key leaders of the Baptist Union. Dates were set. Somehow, a mission in Moscow would be made possible.

*   *   *

I am on a plane. The last time I wrote that, it was the 29th January and it was our first flight of the year. Now it's the 27th November, and we're on a flight from Moscow to Heathrow airport, returning from what may well be our last flight of the year (depending on whether we get to go to the Netherlands). Incidentally, every page of this book so far has been written on this or that flight to somewhere or other, during the last year.

It has been a turbulent year. We have now been to 29 out of the 30 cities the Lord gave us to visit four years ago, when it all seemed so impossible. Yet we came through cancer and more – and now have 23 cities committed to doing a mission next year, starting in just over two months, with the remainder still thinking about it.

How can one summarise a year like this? It has been an

extraordinary sweep through the world, filling our hearts with a sense of the identity and essence of the 'world church' that few can have had the privilege of experiencing. It is a church in which so many of the problems, challenges and glories are shared. It is – to my surprise – more alike than different, all over the world. And the 'powers and principalities' it has to face are more comparable, from one country or continent to the other, than I would have dreamt to be the case. Materialism, consumerism, liberalism in morals, the attack on the family, pornography – all these forces the church is having to contend with in each of the countries we visited. One tide of evil seems to be sweeping the face of the earth and the church must learn to stand together in order to be able to fight it. 'No man is an island.' Nor is the church in any one country.

But the children of God are able to recognise the voice of God in every country and across every culture. Somehow, virtually all were able to see this vulnerable initiative as from the Lord. That is quite an extraordinary confluence of thought and response, across such a variety of cultures and nations. Truly, there is one church, one Lord and one voice of the Spirit, heard by all – a tremendously encouraging fact. And everywhere we went, we were 'family', with a love and sense of commitment that no other grouping on earth could begin to match.

We observed real variety in the different nations, but also some disturbing sameness. It's odd to travel the globe and see that 'local dress', so much a feature of life not so long ago, is rapidly becoming a thing of the past. In Egypt, India and Nigeria, a significant proportion of people (but always less than half) wore local dress. We saw a handful of people wearing ponchos in Colombia; in Moscow they wore furs, but the cold may have had something to do with that! Apart from that, it's all jeans and trainers, T-shirts with American themes or other forms of Western fashion. It has covered the globe. It is actually quite sad to go from Tokyo to Beijing, Tel Aviv to Istanbul, Santiago to Nairobi and see everyone dressed virtually the same. Of course, capitals will tend to be more global in their outlook than their country's hinterlands, but the trend is clear. The West – in its fashions, its films, its music, its values, its deep problems – is sweeping all before it. We had thought that the church in the UK faced problems perhaps also faced by other Western countries; but we actually face problems assailing the whole world.

Our heart is to see the church grow into its oneness – and find therein a strength it will never have while it is divided and parochial. We need to see Christ, and to do so is to see the world church, his body on earth, as he sees it: which is surely as being connected, as the different parts of any body must be in order to function properly.

I have been struck that this mad project could probably not have been mounted even a decade earlier. Email and the internet have been of crucial importance in the mechanics of doing what we have been doing. Relatively cheap flights have also been a boon. Doing this from any base other than an English-speaking one would also have been almost impossible. The world speaks English, and all around the world we were able to function without difficulty in our native language, with the exception of the Spanish-speaking world. So an Englishman married to a Nicaraguan would do fine!

England, our home country, which we represent abroad, has probably impacted the 30 countries concerned more than any other country. Of those 30 countries, 12 have been British-ruled, and another 13 have been allies or (more often) enemies in wars, mostly in living memory. That's 25 out of 30. Quite a tally! Of the others, three are in the Hispanic world, with which Gina has an instinctive rapport. Only two – the Philippines and Indonesia – are not covered by the factors mentioned above. So we found ourselves treading, and renewing, an existing path of relationship from our country almost everywhere we went.

Part 4

14

Will It, Won't It?

2005. This was the year the Lord had given us – to do this extraordinary, unprecedented sweep of the main capitals of the world. Most of it was in place at the beginning of the year (and China and Japan got confirmed through repeat visits in January). All was ready.

Or was it? What was really in store for us? None of the missions were what you might call 'secure'. In China, for example, a delightful elderly man, one of the doyens of the underground church whom we amazingly got to meet, simply said, 'I don't know how we can do this here; but I do feel the kingdom of God coming in this – so come.' We duly bought tickets to come. Russia was just about as insecure. How might it be done there? Our tickets for a team of eleven had already been bought when word started to seep out that the original group was backing out of the mission. The Baptist Union, however, remained interested. Could it somehow be pulled together?

It wasn't just the difficult places which carried uncertainty. Would people, in whichever country, fulfil their promises, get permission in time, and indeed raise the money needed to pay for the mission? After all – and this is key – we were not, are not, famous. There was never the pull of a 'big name' coming, which would in itself galvanise the local churches into concerted action and give them the incentive to perform that comes from being part of something impressive. On the contrary, as far as they were concerned, this was an unproven concept (never attempted in their culture), with a financial cost (quite unusual in so many countries where Western missionary organisations routinely pay for everything) and a risk factor associated with taking it on. The only people who would do this would surely be those who, like the man in China, saw something of the kingdom of God in it and wanted to take it on for that reason alone. That could give the project immense strength – the strength of being backed by people of courage and vision, who couldn't be in it for anything except the right reasons. On the other hand, it might limit the number of other leaders on whom they could count for support; and, being a venture of faith for all concerned, it really needed God to *act* to make it come good.

So would he? Did he?

I want to tell you what actually happened – whether the missions did happen or not, whether they did work in vastly different cultures or not, whether the money came in or not, whether the sense of expectation we had about the year was to be matched by the acts of God that would undoubtedly be required to see it through.

You carry a vision; you communicate it to others more or less successfully; then they look to *you* to deliver what *you* promised. Lord, please help us! Please come with us, or we simply don't want to go.

*   *   *

I won't give you a blow-by-blow account of the missions during 2005. There were too many of them to do that. But there are some themes I want to draw out from what happened in that momentous year.

The first of these themes is summed up by the title of this chapter, 'Will It, Won't It?' In several missions, we found ourselves in situations of total weakness where *we could do nothing* to get out of the hole in which we found ourselves.

I want to give you two examples of this and tell you what happened. The very first hole came with the very first mission destination – South Africa.

You gear up mentally for the first mission – the first of the world capitals, the first part of the supposed fulfilment of this vision carried for years. You arrive in the country – and it becomes apparent that everything in terms of organisation is a bit up in the air. . . In particular, there seemed to have been a mix-up about when and where the training evening would be, switches having been made at the last moment. At any rate, at 7.00 p.m. (the start time), nobody, but nobody, had turned up.

This started quite a black hour for me. Where were the 60 leaders who had greeted the vision so enthusiastically a year and a half before? Had they even been invited? Was this, the first of the capital city missions, to fail before it had even started? What of all that vision? What of that sense of a large canvas on which the Lord was painting something so very special? Was this how it was to be converted into reality, here on the ground in Johannesburg/Pretoria? I walked around the church grounds, effectively nursing a broken heart.

After about half an hour, two cars rolled in. Gradually a few more people arrived. Eventually, by 8.00 p.m., there were 35 people there in addition to the team of ten from the UK and Germany (Heinrich and Sabine, leaders of the German OTM, were there). But the damage was done to my soul. How could I get up before that small grouping and speak of the vision the Lord had given me in 2000? Could I carry conviction? Did I have any left? It was just like Manchester 2000 – a disastrous start to the big city missions of that year, with the almost empty hall and a call to impart the vision I felt the Lord had given me. And yet . . . Manchester had turned out all right, hadn't it? And that year had progressed wonderfully from such a difficult start.

It was the sight of three babies in the audience (no – they weren't part of the count of 35 team members) that gave me a starting point in which my heart could engage – a message about small beginnings. Who could tell what those vulnerable young lives would accomplish in the future? In the same way, God was beginning something that *would grow*.

Well, it worked for me, anyway!

Small though the team was, at least most of those at the Pretoria training evening, including five pastors, said they would also come and serve in Sophiatown (where we were also to do a mission – the one on the fiftieth anniversary of the black population having been expelled). There was equally the hope that there would be a follow-through from Sophiatown into Pretoria, in the same way.

The Sophiatown mission started beautifully. For the first evening, it was based in the grounds of a white Dutch Reform church. The barbecues were there and, eventually, so was the food. A genuinely mixed team of about 70 went about their tasks in a lovely spirit. Everyone was aware that something special was happening. The churches had never worked together before and there was a wonderful feeling of *natural* unity between black, white and coloured. We were simply enjoying being one church together and no great effort had to be put into that. It was something the Lord was accomplishing in our midst. The worship was wonderful.

One young black man – a guest at the barbecue – asked me where the toilets were. I went up to another young man, a member of the host church, and asked if he could kindly show him where the toilets were. You could see the momentary hesitation on his face. It was a taboo-busting moment as he took his young black friend into the smart white church to use the toilets.

The next evening, the mission moved to a predominantly black area in front of the 'Police Flats'. The children crowded round and again there was an atmosphere of great joy. We estimate that during the two evenings of mission in Sophiatown, about 200 people came forward to receive Christ. Many more were impacted by the general sense of breakthrough and were touched in their hearts to see black, white and coloured working together so joyfully and naturally. All this on the exact fiftieth anniversary of the 'removals'.

The next night, it was supposed to be the first of three days of mission in Pretoria. But, by the time we returned from Sophiatown to our lovely hotel, it had become clear that the mission in Pretoria was lost. Permission from the authorities to do the mission had only been sought the day before it was due to start! The local authority had said that no parks or public spaces whatsoever could be used without a minimum of 14 days to achieve permission – fair enough, really. The one Pretoria-based church that was trying to move things forward had therefore decided to bow out.

Michelle, a lovely coloured lady from Sophiatown, had held out some hope that her contacts could produce something. Yet there was nowhere we could do the mission, even if Michelle's contacts came up trumps. Gina urged me to let go. This I found intensely difficult to do. The first of the capital cities . . . and we were to fall at the first fence? Eventually, finally, I did let go – and told the Lord that it was his mission. Yet it was a forlorn group of Europeans who had dinner together that night back at the hotel.

*   *   *

The next morning, a message came through from Michelle that she had got something! What had happened was this. She had phoned five contacts in Pretoria (I think none of them were church leaders), asking them to make suggestions as to who might help. They had come back with a total of eleven suggested contacts. She had then literally prayed through the whole night.

As she looked at the list, one name jumped out at her. In the morning, she tried to phone but got no answer. Convinced that the Holy Spirit was pointing her towards this one contact, she resisted phoning the others, waited, then phoned again and now got an immediate response: 'That sounds great – and we have a big church garden where it could happen, *without needing official permission.*'

When we moved to the hotel in Pretoria (previously booked) and proceeded to look up where the church – our mission site – might be in this city of two million people, it turned out to be just round the corner – less than 100 metres from our hotel. It is signs like this that let you know that it's all right; it will be fine; it's all in hand. By the way, the church turned out to have on its premises chairs, tables and – wait for it – barbecues!

We lost the first night of mission there, but used the time profitably to meet the pastor, the youth pastor, about 30 members of the worship group (who all became enthusiastic team members), a couple of other churches nearby – and then the church we had originally been working with, which also turned out to be around the corner. A mission team was formed. By the second day the mission was ready to roll, having been pulled together from scratch at 24 hours' notice. The site was ideal. Again, we saw about 200 people come forward to receive Christ. Local leaders and others from Johannesburg and Sophiatown were astonished at the atmosphere – that typical atmosphere that seems always to be there with one of these missions, and that seems to draw people in, in a spirit of grace and joy.

I particularly remember one young man. The barbecue was nearly drawing to a close and I felt drawn (the only way to describe it) to go out of the grounds of the church and invite once more. I walked towards the main street, met this young man and said, 'Can I invite you to a free barbecue?' Then I added, 'It's just over there; I'll take you there.' I don't know why I said that – I never volunteer to take someone there personally! We walked together towards the barbecue site. As we arrived at the entrance, I introduced him to Helen, one of our UK team members. She invited him in, but a sort of terror seemed to have come over him. Helen, a gentle lady, comforted and reassured him. Meanwhile, I got Gina (as I usually do when I'm out of my depth). She arrived, saw what was happening and started to pray for this young man, and felt led to deliver him from various spirits, including a spirit of fear, rejection and other things besides.

Peace came over him. Now in the church grounds, he spoke to David and confessed that he was a male prostitute and he knew this to be abominable to God. David counselled him and reassured him of the forgiveness available to him – and all of us, whatever we've done – in Christ, and finally, after many tears, he led him to the Lord. The man still wondered how he could live, after giving up his source of income. But his face was changed and peace had completely filled him. David then introduced him to a local pastor, who took him under his wing. I was so very moved to see what had come out of a simple instinct to go and invite (as it turned out) one more person. It reminds me of the parable of the shepherd who leaves the 99 sheep to seek out the one lost sheep. God cares so deeply for each individual.

*   *   *

It is strange how, while accepting that when we are weak we are strong, we tend to do everything in our power to avoid situations of weakness. So, in my experience, God forces them on us. So it was when I resigned my job and found that the redundancy settlement was denied me; so it was when we were trying to recover that money in court.

Again, when I was about to travel around the world to impart the vision for missions in 30 capital cities, I was found to have cancer – and had to continue making arrangements for the following year without knowing whether I would be alive to see it through. I find that those are the times in which God moves the most – it's just that he usually has to put us in those circumstances against our will, because we'll never opt to go there voluntarily! I guess this is the key. When you do find yourself there, have the faith and expectancy to think that God is doing something, that it will be all the better for this weakness in the end, rather than kicking over the traces, complaining that all is lost and giving up (and thus acquiring an example for the future about how faith doesn't work)!

South Korea is the other example I want to give of this 'will it, won't it?' tendency. Seoul gave the 2005 missions roller-coaster ride some of its steepest aspects – both up and down. And up again. And. . .

This was a mission of contradictions between the apparent and the actual. At one level, in this place of Christian revival in the 1970s, it was as strong as it could get. The Association of Christian Churches in Anyang, with no less than 600 churches in membership from this satellite town of greater Seoul, was fully behind the mission. The chairman was beside us on the mission every day. But how many churches were actually involved in anything other than name? Perhaps ten – max! And what about team members? Well – there had been a massive misunderstanding. We said we wanted worship bands and they called in the Korean gospel music association, with about 20 top musicians taking part; singers with magnificent tenor voices, a Christian heavy metal band (highly professional at that); a lorry that unfolded into a professional stage; about 100 chairs, arranged theatre-style; a tin-foil-wrapped snack – but nothing that would attract people, no invitation cards, and virtually no ordinary church members at all.

In the event, we effectively cancelled the On the Move mission for the first night and just let the performance take place as organised. Afterwards, I took the leaders aside. We wanted to be fully appreciative of all the hard work that had been done, and of the excellence of what they had put forward. It was only that we specifically wanted to show them On the Move and pass onto them what the Lord was doing through *this* kind of mission. I had to present once again, in simple form, the vision for On the Move. I explained that it was about mobilising ordinary church members, about simple worship and close engagement with people over a meal.

Day Two started with training. We now had around 40 Korean team members – a lot better. We had invitation cards too. I got a bunch of Koreans to volunteer to sing in a worship band. Nick gathered them around him at the church where we were doing the training and, with his guitar, led them in a rendition of 'Jesus loves me, this I know' (in Korean, of course). The joy and sense of release as ordinary church members took on the mantle of worship was palpable. They were magnificent!

Then we went onto the streets. A handful of the professional musicians were there again, setting up, and the 'ordinary' ones just melted away. I was so disappointed. Please don't get me wrong: I have nothing against professional musicians (let alone competent ones). They can add *massively.* It's just that the release of the Spirit comes, as we see again and again, when ordinary believers are released in worship. God must just love what they do, because the Spirit comes every time – and conversions happen. The only thing I know that can kill an On the Move mission stone dead is when good musicians 'perform'. There seems to be a simplicity and freedom that many good musicians find it difficult to move in. A couple of good musicians, anchoring a bunch of ordinary singers and *serving* them, is what I look for ideally. The difference, in terms of the results of the mission, is enormous.

So our ordinary Korean singers had melted away; we also still had no tables; the food was still not right; but at least we did have some ordinary team members and a good position in the main street. But, without tables, there was little interaction between team members and guests. It still wasn't really On the Move.

There are moments when I get unreasonable. I'm like a dog with a bone. I just won't let go of the vision – until I feel in my spirit that what we came for has been fulfilled in that place. With a tenacity that I believe was God-inspired, I was unable to give up on the missing elements. We needed tables! We needed attractive food! Was I pushing too hard? I so much wanted them to see what God would do when we were true to what he had shown us.

Now, as I've stressed from our experience, God's strength is truly made perfect in our weakness. It is sometimes when we come to the end of what *we* can do that the Lord bares his mighty right arm. It happened here, *par excellence.* Listen to this. Day Three came. So much more now came together. The food was much better (following a deal with the

Korean equivalent of the local sausage sizzler). And we had tables (oh, victory of victories!). But there were two un-expected problems. First, the PA system that we'd had the day before didn't show up, so it was impossible to do any-thing from the front, in terms of preaching. Second, *it was raining*.

I guess I was philosophical, but definitely sad. This was to have been the day – the very last opportunity – on which we could show them On the Move at its best and demon-strate its true character and values. They were already in the process of setting up a Korean OTM organisation and so I felt it was extremely important that they should really *understand* what they were taking on. With the rain, only small groups of people sat huddled together under umbrel-las, and only 100 or so guests joined us through the whole evening, compared to the 1,000 we might have attracted in that position in the main street. Two thirds of our lovely tables were empty! And we couldn't preach, due to the absence of the PA system. I had to give it up to the Lord: 'You know best.' So, with our lovely Korean singers, whom we did finally marshal into a vibrant worship group, we set-tled down to just praising God – in the rain. There's a release that sometimes comes in adversity, a joy that breaks through when nothing seems to matter any more. Anyway, we went for it – finally, just our team of eight from the UK, worshipping, smiling, veritably leaping about in rhythm, all in the rain and soaked to the skin. It didn't seem like any kind of victory at the time. It was only when eight o'clock arrived, and we packed our instruments away, that we found out what God had actually accomplished.

He had, in fact, accomplished three things that were

sovereign acts of grace. First, there were conversions – and not just a few. I started to be handed response cards. I counted. There were 19, virtually all representing conversions. I couldn't believe it. All this in the rain, with no PA system, and just a small team of Korean Christians sitting at the tables with a diminutive number of guests? Amazing fruit! But then more response cards were passed to me – and more, and more. My momentary disbelief (did these include the ones for the previous two days? No, they didn't) started to turn to increasing excitement. The final tally was no less than 60 response cards, representing close on 60 conversions – an astonishing outcome, a miraculous outcome, which was more than I had imagined by a factor of about 20. I still find it hard to believe that this was achieved by means of ordinary Korean believers, in such adverse circumstances, amongst such a small number of guests, in the rain.

The second remarkable thing was that the circumstances which I had so lamented – no PA, the rain, etc. – had become the very tools that God used to convince the Korean leaders beyond doubt *why* it had worked so spectacularly. If you have an inclination towards using professional singers and a 'from the front' style of ministry, putting your best foot forward, and if you then see the complete absence of anything 'from the front', coupled with the stunning success of a small group of Christians sitting at tables in the rain, ministering one-to-one to the needs of our guests, with only a bunch of ordinary Christians, soaked the skin with acoustic guitars and a lot of joy, doing the worship – well, then a vital point is massively proven. The leaders could not stop talking about it. They had grasped *in their hearts* (the hardest place to reach) that this was about ordinary Christians going out in weakness in the power of the Holy Spirit, released through true worship. They had completely caught the vision.

Third, as the local leaders embraced the English team at the close of the mission, all of us looking like drowned rats, we saw that we had in fact won their hearts by what we had done – that they *loved* us for our perseverance and joy in adversity and willingness just to serve, in these very inglorious circumstances. They simply loved us – and we them.

So it was that the Korean On the Move was joyfully born, in an official ceremony the following evening. The mission received quite a lot of press coverage and enquiries were already coming in from various cities.

15

The Presence of God

Most of the missions in 2005 were in fact well organised, well understood by the locals, and completely devoid of heart-stopping moments! Most were a delight. But that didn't make us any less dependent on the Lord – we were just dependent in a different way. Without the presence of God, the formula would amount to little more than music and sausages (or paella . . . or 'barbecued cow meat' as they called it in Nigeria).

New Zealand is a good case in point. There were 17 of us from the UK this time. The Wellington churches, which had never worked together before (and the pastors we met hadn't even known who their counterparts were), in fact came together wonderfully – 16 churches in all. There were about 150 team members at the training evening and the priority seemed to be to lift their faith level. As we fed 2,700 people over three days, the impact of the mission served to increase *my* faith level. What we saw, as never before, was how a society which had left Christian values far behind and truly embraced an 'anything goes' culture could be captured once again by the gospel. I'm not referring here to the number of conversions (with about a dozen recorded, and perhaps five times that number guessed at, but nothing compared to Africa). What I'm referring to is the 'feel' of the city, which seemed to move from pagan and oppressive to light and shining in the space of three days. When, on the first day, two young men held up placards announcing that 'God is dead' and the like, it already looked pathetic, rather than threatening. And, as the sense of God's presence deepened, there was really no 'proud obstacle to the name of Jesus' that could be lifted on those days. The city felt 'ours'. The street people and, apparently, the police too commented on the different atmosphere pervading the city. The unity between the churches was effortless. As I walked down the streets on the last evening, past the sex shops, the crystal shops and all the other spiritual nasties, I felt I had the authority to declare that their time had come and that they would close down. The main local leader said afterwards that the mission had led him to reassess how far one simply had to bow to the present culture, and how far we as a church could actually say, 'Thus far and no further.'

In Australia, the first day of the mission was marred by rain – but the rain in fact only served to confirm the servant hearts of the team of about 150 from perhaps 15 churches. The adversity (not for the first time) produced an infectious joy that remained a hallmark of the mission. A member of the public, a senior government scientist with whom I spoke for an hour, kept saying, 'I've been an atheist all my life; but what these people have is the real thing and I want it. I would smell a rat if there was one, but there's no rat here.' As the five worship bands filled the centre of Canberra with praise, one could start to imagine, as one team member said, Canberra being Christ's. And with that imagination could come the faith to ask for it and see it through.

I was reminded of the verse in Luke 10 where the 72 ordinary people whom Jesus sent out to minister the kingdom came back 'with joy'. Jesus said, 'I saw Satan fall like lightning' (v. 18). I take this as meaning that, as the ordinary believers started to exercise *their* ministry, Satan lost his position of authority in that place – because he only ever had authority on the basis of a lie, that we are 'under his thumb'. The minute that believers discover the deception (Satan is the great deceiver) and start to move with the authority they actually have in Christ, the situation is reversed. And Jesus' very next statement is this: 'I have given you authority to trample on snakes and scorpions and to overcome all the power of the enemy' (v. 19). The turning point is when we discover that it really *is* so. And 'we' means the simple, ordinary ones. As Jesus goes on to say, 'I praise you, Father . . . because you have hidden these things from the wise and learned, and revealed them to little children . . . for this was your good pleasure' (v. 21). I'm convinced that it still is. The church, in the shape of the ordinary church members mobilised for mission, has very much more authority than it realises.

This same sense of the presence of God we had also known in the UK – perhaps as powerfully as elsewhere.

But in English missions (and in Anglo-Saxon countries like Australia, New Zealand or Canada) it takes the team at least a day to settle into the mission and begin to be bold. And in England, members of the public are so fearful of somehow being manipulated into doing something they don't want to do, that a childlike response to the gospel is nigh-on impossible for them, even though they are being profoundly touched. In many countries, however, we started seeing a different pattern. The presence of God yielded so much tangible fruit! In Brasilia, for example, the team of about 170 were so up for it that response cards were being handed to me in a steady stream from the first five minutes of the mission. As for the general public, when we did an appeal and asked people to put their hands up if they had prayed the prayer, a veritable forest of hands would go up and many dozens of them would come forward in an improvised altar call, African style. Likewise in Nairobi, large numbers came and we know of about 400 who professed a new faith (and filled in response cards) during the three lunchtimes. There was a harmony and an ease about these missions which made them a delightful experience. And what a harvest! It was so easy. There was always a powerful sense of the anointing and direction of the Holy Spirit when we preached. Yet it is worth noting that, even in lands becoming used to revival, the pastors were always amazed at what they were witnessing. It was the sense of God's presence that they remarked on, which made the atmosphere so loving and evangelism so easy. This verdict was echoed all over the world.

I do believe that we have come into a new era for

evangelism. Once it may have been a more intellectual, propositional affair – at least in the UK. Now the move of the Spirit that was evidenced in Toronto and other places in the 1990s seems to me to have produced a sense of anointing that is widely *felt* and that produces an atmosphere wherever the Holy Spirit is free to move. That was surely the case during the times when the Bible speaks of the presence of God, of his glory filling the temple and his people impacted in various ways by the move of the Spirit. It is certainly the case now. Evangelism consists in allowing the Holy Spirit free rein, and then reaping the fruit of his sweet impact on people, quite as much as it consists in initiating conversations or presenting a case to them. Not that the case is unimportant; it's just that the process seems increasingly to start elsewhere – with the Spirit touching the heart first and the mind second. For, as Paul says (in 2 Corinthians 2:15–17):

> We are . . . the aroma of Christ among those who are being saved and those who are perishing. To the one we are the smell of death; to the other, the fragrance of life. And who is equal to such a task? Unlike many, we do not peddle the word of God for profit. On the contrary, in Christ we speak before God with sincerity, like men sent from God.

These missions, with the emphasis on worship, love, generosity, prayer ministry and the aroma or atmosphere of the presence of God, are providing a deeply impactful *experience* of God's presence. Into that shared experience, we – the ordinary believers with sincerity of heart and a generous spirit – can then speak with remarkable results. As you 'tell them the kingdom of God is near' (Luke 10:9), you are confirming something they are already perceiving and clarifying something which is already evoking their heartfelt response.

*   *   *

Japan is, as I said, such a bound country. Evangelical Christians make up about 0.3 per cent of the population, the churches feel very hard pressed and see little fruit from their evangelistic efforts. This is hard ground and Japanese people, steeped in a mixture of Buddhism, Shintoism and capitalism, are hard to reach, to say the least. One missionary told us that she had worked with lots of churches in Japan and that if a church sees one conversion in a year, it's a miracle.

Yet God was giving us words about a harvest, about streams in the desert. How might his presence irrigate such a . . . well . . . desert?

Our mission turned out to be with one small church. By small, I mean about 20 members. A handful of them were able to join us for the mission. Other churches had shown interest (four pastors came to see and take part), but none had been willing to risk their flocks on an unknown venture of this sort, with no evidence that it would work in Japan. The Japanese are a cautious people. Pastor Miyamoto, a glorious exception to this, had managed to mobilise his team which, together with eight from England, numbered about 25.

The park where we had permission to be was lovely, but fairly empty – which in a sense was just as well, given our tiny team. We could not attend properly to many guests! In the event, about 60 guests were handed a sandwich each day, and the majority of them sat down in ones, twos and threes on the stone steps of a type of amphitheatre, with some of the UK team and other singers and musicians from Japan and a variety of other countries (it was interesting choosing songs!) standing on the stage, worshipping God – with a clapped-out PA system, but with real freedom and joy too. It wasn't hard worshipping at all. Again, there was that sense of the presence of God. Team members sat with guests, many received prayer (amazing in itself) and each day we received a steady flow of reports of real conversions. One guest was the husband of a Christian, and got our team member to phone his wife to tell her the great news that, at last, he had given his life to Christ too. An elderly couple kept saying that the music was changing their hearts. They just drank in the atmosphere and readily gave their lives to Christ when the gospel was explained to them. Others were ready to come to church, to find out more, to engage in Bible study and seek the meaning of what they had seen. Altogether, we know of 14 who gave their lives to Christ, and many others who wanted further contact.

Pastor Miyamoto was so excited by what he was witnessing, and kept on commenting on the 'real changes', the 'faces changed' and the 'Holy Spirit moving'. Both he and the other pastors who had come to see truly grasped the dynamics of what was happening and were amazed by the openness of ordinary Japanese people, in the context of the worship and the presence of God it ushered in, and the chance to engage with people over a simple meal. So, small

though it was, it was in many ways a triumphant mission –
again, born of great weakness, and of the significant
courage shown by a very small Japanese church in going for
it, come what may. They invited us to come back in 2006,
confident that, now it was proven, many churches would
want to take part. And next time, they told us, it would be
a barbecue!

*   *   *

Abuja, Nigeria, couldn't have been more different. There
is a large church-going population there. Our training
evening was attended by 200 people from about 30
churches. A total of 700 dear souls (actually including a
good many Muslims) came forward over the three
evenings to give their lives to Christ. Again, as in the other
African missions, each one was then prayed for individually – rewarding and infinitely worthwhile, but exhausting
too. For each one we also got a response card, to enable
proper follow-up. Still used to UK missions, I found it
extraordinary to look out over that dusty, rubbish-strewn
clearing in the middle of an African shanty town on the
edge of Abuja, packed with people of a vastly different
culture, on a steamy hot evening under the lights rigged
up to illuminate this evening mission. The choir of about
50 team members was in full voice, belting out gospel
tunes and worship numbers with an enthusiasm and an
infectious joy that would lift any spirit. And yet, here in
this vastly different setting, was an On the Move mission
that *still* felt just like an On the Move mission always
did. There was, unmistakeably, *that* atmosphere – the

atmosphere that accompanies every mission. It was in so many respects utterly different from the missions we had been used to, and yet in the most important respects it was completely the same.

16

War in the Heavenly Places

Sometimes, as in Korea or Japan, God 'just did it' in spite of our best plans and our efforts to get a handle on what was going on. We just had to carry on and, at some point or other, the mist would clear and we would realise how great the advance had actually been.

There have been other kinds of advances, too – those based on the conscious application of what tends to be called 'spiritual warfare'. I want to highlight three of these, in three great European capitals, Rome, Madrid and Paris. They have shown us powerfully the relevance of Paul's dictum that 'our struggle is not against flesh and blood, but against the rulers, against the authorities, against the powers of this dark world and against the spiritual forces of evil in the heavenly realms' (Ephesians 6:12). It is these experiences that confirm to me how, in all cases, when the breakthrough comes, we should be thanking God and not looking to our own achievement.

Not many weeks before the Rome mission in May, it fell

apart as we received a two-line email from the people who had agreed to organise it (knowing we had bought air tickets) to the effect that it was off, maybe some other time. . . But one small church (found for us by an Italian friend in Lyon, France!) agreed to work with us. And so, with a team of 14 (but not David and Barbara, who had come back from the Far East absolutely exhausted, not surprisingly, given that David is in his sixties), we arrived for a mission in Frascati, on one of the hills of Rome – an upmarket area with delightful views and a simply wonderful villa-style hotel.

Again, rather like Japan, it was a church of about 20 members. They nearly all turned out for the training evening and were much encouraged by the talk, which emphasised what happens when we go out in weakness. (Well, it would, wouldn't it?) Even at short notice, they had managed to get permission for a mission in Frascati for the Saturday night, but the attempt to do something similar in a neighbouring town on the Friday evening was still in the balance. In the event, as we met on the Friday in the piazza of that town, it turned out that permission had been refused. The mission was off. We were down to one day only, in Frascati itself. Again, this was disappointing. But what would God bring from it all? There is always this sense (this experience, really) that God must be *doing something*. . . It didn't take us too long to find out what.

In lieu of doing mission that evening (as we had all geared up to do), we decided to decamp to the church and have a time of worship and prayer together. After we had sung a few choruses, the American founder of the church decided to brief us about the history of Frascati. He told us that no evangelical church had ever been successfully planted there, even though some had tried. Now this one, with 20 members, was trying to establish itself in the community. But Frascati was widely recognised to be the regional centre for Satanism in that part of Italy; significantly, Frascati (of all places) had also been adopted as the national headquarters of the German military command and of the Gestapo in the Second World War; and it was in Frascati that the Pope who went on to found the Inquisition had been born and raised. What a collection of dodgy antecedents for one small town! No wonder it was so difficult.

We had some background in this. I told you how the history of Tonbridge (one of our early missions) hung over the town generations later. Most remarkably, Gina once had a vision as we were preparing for the north of England mission in 2003. She saw a female figure, dressed in white, first in a cave and then walking across the hills. A local pastor she subsequently shared this with said, 'I know who that is.' He explained how an Irish female saint in the ninth century had travelled to Cumbria, lived in a cave and walked the hills bringing spiritual revival wherever she went. Now, what can create a 'spiritual stronghold' even out of a godly ministry is what people do with it afterwards. In other words, it can be turned into idolatry and therefore become a spiritual snare to the people. Why? Because it creates an alternative focus for devotion (diverting the faithful from Jesus) and this becomes spiritually crippling, even to subsequent generations, because in fact 'there is no other name under heaven given to men by which we must be saved'

(Acts 4:12). An alternative focus leads believers to 'bark up the wrong tree', as it were.

Well, on the way back from talking to the local pastor, we decided to do some 'spiritual warfare' and, with Gina doing the driving, I took authority and out loud in Jesus' name broke the power of this stronghold over Cumbria. That prayer took no more than 60 seconds. It was during that 60 seconds that something snapped in the mechanism of our car, and suddenly only two out of the five gears could be engaged. Uncanny! But these things do happen and you learn to cope with them and see something of the unseen spiritual world in their operation. As it happens, on our return to Birmingham we heard that the towns of White-haven, Barrow-in-Furness and Kendal had all independently agreed to do the mission *on that very day*, upping the Cumbria total from two to five.

I later related this story to Roger Mitchell, the friend who had taken me to Dallas years before. It turned out that he had been having a prayer meeting with a small group in Cumbria on the very same day, in which they got to grips with key things in the spiritual realm over that county and felt they had 'made history'. The vision Gina had; the closely matching explanation from the local pastor; the gears snapping as I prayed; three towns saying 'yes' the same day; the prayer meeting Roger Mitchell had the same day: were these coincidences? I very much doubt it.

Now, in Frascati, it seemed to us that something over the city had to be broken. It also seemed that we knew why the mission in another town that night had not gone ahead. Before plundering a strong man's house, said Jesus, you first have to bind the strong man. That was God's agenda for that evening, and then the next day's mission would be able to go ahead unhindered. As we sat there in the garden of this church, Gina had one of her prophetic moments. She stood up, said 'I don't usually do this', and proceeded to gather with her feet the dirt from the ground beneath her. She made a pile of it, and then said, 'As I am gathering the dirt from this garden, I believe that God is gathering the debris of the history of Frascati; as he gathers this, he is sending his fire to burn it up and cleanse it and give the town a new start.' Now, there was such an anointing on Gina as she said these words that you could have cut the atmosphere with a knife. As she mentioned that God was sending his fire, I happened to open my eyes and saw – blazoned across the sky – a fiery sunset at the moment of its greatest intensity. A couple of minutes later it was gone. But what was not gone was the sense we all had that God had spoken. I prayed at this point something I had never prayed before – that the mission would *double the size* of that church of 20 people.

Are you sceptical about all of this – sunsets and all? I wouldn't be surprised if you were. By instinct, in some ways I am too. The fruit of that mission wasn't immediately there to see. We had a sense of openness, sure enough, and the little church felt accepted by its community for the first time. But the numbers that came to the park were smallish (about 250) by virtue of the fact that the barbecue site was five or ten minutes' walk from the piazza where we invited people. There were three conversions, a lovely atmosphere – but nothing too special. What *was* special was the phone conversation I had nine days later with the assistant pastor at the church. 'Guess how many people we had in church yesterday?' he asked me. Then he spilt the beans. 'Forty-three!' he said.

*   *   *

I was hesitant about writing this next bit about Madrid. But since Nicholas, my 15-year-old son, just interrupted me in my writing on this flight (from Mexico City to Washington DC two weeks after the Madrid mission – our children are with us for the North America trip) specifically to ask me if I was including this spiritual warfare bit and to say 'I think you should', I will take it as a word from the Lord, and plunge in.

In advance of the mission, we were on a tourist bus tour of Madrid. The commentator said, 'This is Cybele Plaza, named after the statue of the goddess Cybele. This statue can be regarded as the symbol of Madrid.' My ears pricked up. Cybele? The symbol of Madrid? Gina and I explained to the two other team members with us that we needed to get off the bus to pray. They came, no doubt curious about what was afoot. I explained to them from scratch our experience of this particular 'goddess'.

Two and a half years before, I told them, we had gone to Lyon to prepare for our mission there. As we prayed, Gina had a picture of birds – many, many large birds, just standing there. Then she had the name 'Diana' in her mind. Gina later asked our local co-ordinator whether the name Diana might mean something in relation to Lyon. He said it did. The Basilica (or cathedral) of Lyon had been built on the site of the Roman temple of Cybele, the god-

dess of fertility, previously known by the Greeks as Diana.
Aha! So we went to the Basilica to pray. Inside the Basilica were probably a hundred statues (one under every
column) of – wait for it – birds; large birds, just standing
there. There was a statue of the Virgin Mary, which
notably depicted her as being seated on a throne with two
lions lying in front of her, one at each side. Tapestries on
the walls depicted the history of the Basilica. Apparently,
Louis XIII had no male heir and had said that, if God
gave him a son, then he would 'give' France to the Virgin
Mary. The subsequent ceremony, in which France was
indeed 'given' to the Virgin Mary, was enacted at that very
Basilica. The son in question became Louis XIV, the 'Sun
King', whose arrogance knew no bounds and who persecuted the Protestants (Huguenots), causing a massive
exodus of over 200,000 of them to other parts of the
world.

It seemed to us (and this is sensitive stuff) that a spiritual
stronghold, built around that goddess Diana and carried on
under the name of Cybele, had manifested itself in later
French history in a Basilica built on the very grounds of the
temple to Cybele, through France being 'given' to the Virgin Mary there – who (through no fault of her own) was
being put in the place of Christ himself, treated almost as a
goddess, you might say – and therefore taking France away
from saving faith in Christ alone. Remember, this is a spirit
that is being manifested. If you give place to a spirit, it has a
hold on you. Imagine our surprise when, on our return
home, we researched Cybele and found that she was always
depicted seated on a throne with two lions lying in front of
her, one on each side. . . What did those architects or

stonemasons think they were doing? What did they *know* they were doing?

At any rate, we prayed against this stronghold in Lyon and had that sense that our prayers were impinging on something highly significant. A wonderful mission followed.

Now, on the tourist bus in Madrid, we were at Cybele Plaza; the statue there depicted the goddess as seated on a throne with two lions in front of her, one on either side; and this statue was to be regarded as 'the symbol of Madrid'. The four of us prayed together, took authority and – as Jesus instructed – bound the spirit.

The evening came and we arrived at the appointed restaurant. (The outdoor mission had to be cancelled at the last minute after the local council 'lost' the permission forms and basically said, 'Tough.') We worshipped and invited on the streets as always – and at 8.00 p.m., the time for the meal, the restaurant was totally empty. Slowly, however, it started to fill up, until finally every table was filled with about 100 people and yet not a single person was without a seat – another extraordinary example of God's hand of planning, when we could do nothing but watch. There were just over 30 from the street, the rest being church members. When we had completed a simple meal, Spanish/English worship and presentations from myself and a Spanish pastor, the local Christians went alongside our guests, talked with them, prayed for them and led them to Christ. By the end, at least ten had given their lives to Christ and nearly all the other 20 or so 'outsiders' had been so taken with the atmosphere, the love and the authenticity of what they

had stumbled on, that they gave their names and addresses and wanted to come to the pastor's church and
learn more about the faith they had for the first time
begun to understand. At least seven were Muslims.

Now, I think that spiritual warfare is meant to be a pre-
cursor to mission. If, before plundering a strong man's
house, one has to bind the strong man (Matthew 12:29),
then by the same token surely the *point* of binding the
strong man is subsequently to plunder his house. The little
mission described above, with an almost unanimous
response from those guests who came, was what followed
in this case.

One rider to this. When we got to the restaurant that
night, Gina noticed the frieze on the massive mirror, taking
up almost half of one side of the restaurant. It was a picture
of Cybele, seated on a throne with two lions in front and
either side of her. Powerless!

*   *   *

The last mission of the year was Paris – and there we found
a number of loose ends tied up, in the spiritual realm at
least. It was in Paris that a key part of the *pattern* of the year
became clear to us.

Paris had been a bugbear ever since the mission scheduled for May had to be abandoned because the local
churches simply could not get permission from the authorities for a barbecue – and they tried a great number of
authorities in many parts of Paris. This had only added to an
already difficult ride in Europe generally. Amsterdam had,
uniquely, never shown interest, while Rome, Moscow and

Madrid had *all* got cancelled before being 'reborn' at the last minute. The same was now happening in Paris.

The week in May when I was trying to rescue the Paris mission had brought a different kind of fruit, though – of long-term significance. We were in Rome (Frascati) at the time. I wondered whether we could find a church in Paris with its own property, on which to hold the barbecue. Then the authorities would have nothing to say about it. This led in my mind to the thought that maybe the Catholic Church could help and, in particular, the Catholic charismatic movement. Well, it so happened that a member of the UK team in Rome with us knew an Englishman who was one of the top leaders of the worldwide Catholic charismatic movement. I was given his phone number. I phoned him up and got to speak to his wife. We certainly connected very well on the phone, and she said that the person who could really help us was the director of the worldwide Catholic charismatic movement in 120 countries. Where was this man based? Well, surprise, surprise – he was in Rome!

I called this senior figure in the international Roman Catholic Church that day and amazingly, when I explained who had given me his name, he agreed to see Gina and myself that very afternoon. He was a delightful man, very eager to help, and he quickly put me onto the leader of the French movement, who was equally charming and helpful.

That particular trail did not produce the hoped-for result for the Paris mission, in spite of real efforts on the part of these Catholic charismatic leaders. But it did strike me as a massively important trail, nonetheless – giving me a real entrée into a huge (but largely separate) world of Roman Catholics who really love the Lord and are open to the Holy Spirit. Just six months before, when visiting Rome the first time, Gina and I had unmistakeably (we felt) discerned God's presence at a service at St Peter's, and I had felt effectively commissioned by the Lord to work to unite this key part of his body of Christ with the Protestant charismatics with whom we were more used to working. I believe the Lord said to me, 'I have many people here,' and that they must be part of the bigger picture as the church learnt to unite. What better way to bring such unity than through mission?

Well, the Paris mission got rescheduled for September and again had to be cancelled because the churches we were working with simply couldn't get permission. It was on the way to India, a month later, that the Lord spoke through a prophecy to the eight UK team members there, saying that he wanted us to pray for the door in Paris to be opened, and that we should pray for this every day for the week that we were together – seven days of prayer, reminiscent of the seven times Joshua marched round Jericho before the walls came tumblin' down!

We did pray, with great fervour and real faith. To what effect? Nothing I could do worked. But Jimmy, our man in Madrid, who was with us a month later in South America, happened to ask, 'Who are your contacts in Paris?' We explained about the situation there. He said, 'I know people in Paris.' Entirely on his own initiative, he travelled to Paris to set things up for us – and a mission was organised for the week before Christmas, in a premier Paris square, the Place de la République. We didn't yet have permission. But, crucially, the church said 'come anyway'.

The morning of the day of mission, our team of eight (including Jimmy) met to pray. We worshipped together. There was a strong anointing on that worship – a special time. We broke bread together.

Then Gina, out of the blue, asked me to explain to the team our understanding of the spiritual stronghold (Cybele) that had previously been so much in evidence in France and Spain. I explained about the statues of birds in the Basilica, the statue of Mary depicted as Cybele, how the 'keys' of France had been given to the Virgin Mary by Louis XIII. But it had not been the true Mary who had received these keys – it had been, we believed, a foul spirit from pre-Christian times, attaching itself to the true Mary, which had received these keys and thereafter used them to subvert the faith of the faithful. It had done so by directing that faith (not innocently, but with intent) away from the God who saves and onto a figure who cannot, continuing an ancient and dark idolatry, but cunningly doing so in a new and seemingly innocent disguise. The result, for the faithful, was a damaging misdirection of their faith, tending towards powerlessness and disappointment – and division from others in the body of Christ. What a 'body blow'!

Was it any surprise, then, that Paris, of all cities, had proved so resistant, consistently saying 'no' to the mission in response to constant applications over twelve months? Here, in Paris, a week before Christmas, I felt I should ask Jimmy (with his Spanish hat on) to bind this stronghold, which he duly did with great anointing and authority.

Immediately, Gina was moved to do another of her prophetic acts. (She really does these quite infrequently!)

She said, 'I see the finger of God pointing at this stronghold of "Mary" and telling it to give up the keys to Paris. And as it does so, I see these keys being put on a pillar.' And then, almost stupidly making a 'pillar' from a handful of pillows in our Paris hotel bedroom where we were praying, she placed a set of keys (my car keys!) on the make-believe pillar and said, 'I believe the Lord wants me to take these keys and give them to you, Martin.' She took them and handed them to me, saying, 'In the name of Jesus, I give you the keys of Paris.'

No more than five seconds after she placed the keys in my hand, the phone rang. What a time for an interruption, we all thought. But it was the secretary of the key church we were working with. They had just received permission from the authorities for 100 church members to do evangelism (yes – real, open evangelism, discussing with people the 'significance of Christmas') in the Place de la République. Extraordinary. After a year of battling and waiting, the breakthrough came just *five seconds* after Gina handed me 'the keys to Paris'.

Meanwhile, my daughter Cristina (in what she described as 'one of the most electric prayer meetings I've ever been in') had just been asking the Lord a series of questions, prompted by a picture in her mind of a large volcano dominating a wide landscape. In her mind she knew that the volcano was Paris and the landscape was Europe – and, somehow, that Paris was the 'key' to Europe. She never really asks questions of God like this, but on this occasion found herself asking, 'How can Paris be the key to Europe?' At that moment, she saw that there was a big round slab of concrete sitting on top of the volcano. Then, in a further vision, she saw a big sledgehammer come and strike this concrete cap, which immediately crumbled. She asked the Lord, 'When is it that the hammer will come down?' The answer arose in her mind: 'It will come down when God *points his finger.'* Her next question was, 'When will God point his finger?' This was immediately followed by Gina saying, 'I see the finger of God pointing at this stronghold of "Mary" and telling it to give up the keys to Paris.' My son-in-law Nick simultaneously had a picture of a volcano erupting in Paris, immediately triggering eruptions of fiery volcanoes in cities across France. (You may be interested to read Luke 11 for Jesus' fascinating account of how he drives out demons 'by the finger of God' [v. 20].)

How many strands were being brought together in one moment! This key stronghold harming and emasculating Catholicism had been challenged in Paris; God had (I believe) commissioned me to work to unite Catholic charismatics and other evangelicals and charismatics while I was in Rome; and then in Rome in May 2005 he had given me contacts at the highest level in the Catholic charismatic world as a direct result of seeking a break-through in Paris. He had led us to the stronghold of Cybele in Lyon, France, and then later in Madrid, Spain – and it was now 'our man in Spain' who was with us as we prayed, and who had, incredibly, managed to open Paris for us.

There was yet one more strand to be discerned. Jimmy had been our closest foreign partner with the capital city missions around the world, coming with us to seven of the capitals. That is, he had been our closest foreign partner with one exception. That exception was Heinrich and

Sabine Baumann and the German On the Move. They and/or their German colleagues had been with us for no less than ten foreign missions that year. No other individuals from any other nation had gone *abroad* with our teams. Then I remembered: the emblem of the 2005 missions, which Gina had painted back in 2003 before anything had yet happened, had featured the flags of 30 nations. The flags had been painted end to end, as if on a long scarf, and that scarf had been draped over a wooden cross, like a letter 'M' – with the two peaks resting, one on each side, on the horizontal bar of the cross, and the middle portion of the 'M' hanging in an arc joining those peaks. (Can you imagine it?) Gina had prayed as she painted, asking God to guide her about where to put each flag. In the centre of the curved part (the middle of the 'M') was the Union flag of the UK. At the two peaks, from which everything else was suspended – the two pivotal positions in the whole design – were the flags of two other countries. All the flags on the left-hand side were suspended from the flag of Germany. All the flags on the right-hand side were suspended from the flag of Spain.

Together, these 'partners in the gospel' were able to stumble on what I believe to be a key to unity in the European church, put asunder 500 years ago in the Reformation. These are big issues and we can only dimly perceive their significance or understand how to handle what we perceive. But Jesus' last recorded prayer is a prayer for unity, and we know that it was and is a matter immensely close to his heart (John 17). Significantly, it is also a prayer for protection, and unity is prayed for in that context: 'Holy Father, protect them by the power of your name – the name you gave me – so that they may be one as we are one' (v. 11). Of all the attacks to be expected, would the greatest be an attack on the unity of the believers? Protection was to be by the power of 'the name you gave me'. 'Jesus' is that name, and it means 'the Lord saves'. Being clear and agreed about *who* alone saves is in fact the key to unity. And that turns out to be the precise area in which this stronghold we have discovered has been operating. Is it not now time to reclaim that unity?

If permission for the Paris mission was received at the precise moment that 'the finger of God' was pointed at this stronghold and the key was passed prophetically, then I believe that we have to regard this permission as but a first-fruit, a pointer to a very much bigger 'open door that no-one can shut' that is now set before us (Revelation 3:8). And the important thing about open doors is to go through them.

So it was that the Paris mission did happen, most fruit-fully, with 100 people on the Place de la République, some of them dressed up as Father Christmas, working all round the square with worship, coffee, hot chocolate and Christ-mas cake, prayer for people's needs and tracts explaining the true significance of the season, and resulting not only in conversions but also in a good many new faces in church the following morning – all with official blessing!

*   *   *

One final example of the 'unearthly' side of mission: in Washington DC we had been let down again by people who had shown great enthusiasm for the mission, had agreed to do it, but thereafter (it emerged) had done absolutely nothing to prepare for it. At the last minute one church, contacted via a trail that started in Frascati, Rome, agreed to work with us.

We duly arrived at the Baptist church on the South East Heights of Washington (the city's second highest point). Kip, the pastor, was delightful, and his (mainly black) congregation were sweet too – or at least the 15 or so that turned up to help with the mission. The evening we had chosen turned out to coincide with a major heatwave, and – just to add to the things against the mission – radios were warning people to stay indoors because of the heat, which reached a whacking 97 degrees and made it that much more difficult to mobilise team members, let alone invite strangers. Nevertheless, Kip fell in wonderfully with our 'we're doing this whatever' attitude. Our team of 13 from England and Germany had to work hard, as we constituted most of the worship band (with myself as the only guitarist), and we had to do pretty much all the preparation and most of the inviting ourselves. Our children and their friends were the star performers in this. As the inviting started, it did get cooler and we seemed fine. About 30 guests had arrived when Kip took the microphone and led a prayer of thanksgiving.

In retrospect, I think what happened next was supernatural – a way of God underlining what he was doing in the unseen realm. As Kip prayed, out of nowhere came a mighty gust of wind – literally hurricane strength. In seconds it had whipped through and stripped away the bunting we had so carefully put up between the trees, and equally suddenly it broke a major branch of dead wood from the big tree above and sent it crashing down right next to us (harmlessly, thank God) – all as Kip was praying. A mighty rushing wind . . . getting rid of 'dead wood' . . . all during this brief prayer. . . These 'coincidences' keep happening!

What was the impact of all this on the mission? Well, our Anglo-German-American worship group just carried on (as always), until the rain came and drove everybody indoors. I was now thinking (not for the first time), 'Lord, what are you doing here?' But as we walked towards the church building, Kip came up to me displaying a singular sort of agitation, and blurted out, 'Martin, this is going to carry on. You have planted a seed that will grow. Now I understand – it's the worship that opens the door to the evangelism. I just led someone to Christ: it was so easy. We're going to do this here, and I'm convener of the other churches in South East, and I will bring this to them as something we must do together. This will continue!' And with a passion that seemed to come from nowhere, On the Move began to be planted in the United States, finding good soil and a conviction that was surprising, especially given the circumstances – namely, being driven indoors by a freak weather system at the very beginning of a barbecue that was having to be abandoned!

Well, it wasn't exactly abandoned. Most of the 30 or so guests followed us indoors, and we improvised our way to a lovely scene in which people chatted at tables and a multinational group of us worshipped with great joy and freedom, in the course of which at least two others gave their lives to Christ (a second being led to the Lord by Kip himself), and four others told him they would be coming to his church. It all simply confirmed the earlier enthusiasm which had landed on him so suddenly. In my heart I do feel that something the Lord has done here will 'go places'.

17

Highs and Lows

You will have got the impression by now that there are considerable difficulties involved in doing what we have been doing. In a sense, I worry that I'm exaggerating the difficulties. It's not that they have been absent, or any less problematic than I've described. It's just that we have found ourselves being carried along by grace – and that at the time it has often (though not absolutely always) seemed less difficult than you might think.

At the mission in the Philippines I was struck by the reaction of Peter, our administrator, who was with us for this trip in November 2005. It was our twenty-first capital city mission (out of 23 that we finally did in the year). All the hallmarks of a 'normal' On the Move foreign mission were there: we never quite knew what the delightful locals had planned or how it would come together; we constantly had to go with the flow of what was happening, knowing that it would turn out all right – because it always did. For Peter, however, this was all new. And so he couldn't stop talking, after the wonderful night of mission in which over 100 people gave their lives to Christ, about the near misses – the brass band that set up to practise 50 metres away from us, drowning out our sound; the late arrival of the equipment and the team members; the lack of people about in the area to invite. We had carried on worshipping anyway (more or less unheard), and then the brass band left just as we were ready to feed people, the team gradually arrived in strength, the atmosphere was wonderful and it all 'just happened'. One young boy who had a constricted chest was prayed for and could immediately, for the first time, breathe normally, which he did with great joy. An 81-year-old man with Parkinson's disease had to be supported by two people to be prayed for, being unable to walk, bend down or even lift his arms. After prayer, he was literally jumping around, bending, raising his arms and demonstrating publicly, to the whole crowd, what God had done for him.

My point is that it had become obvious to Gina, me, Nick and Cristina that it would work out. Peter's excitement at its doing so reminded me how much we had come to assume – and how much we must all have grown in faith and (more or less) peace in the midst of such regular happenings.

So there were extraordinarily tricky moments, which in retrospect look as though they must have been agony to go through. But, with one or two exceptions, they weren't. As you get used to this way of things, and learn to trust in the midst of them, you find that a lot of the time you can keep your balance and not be too preoccupied with the dangers of falling.

One good example of this came in Mexico. We arrived, and it turned out that nothing had been arranged. We were, however, taken to meet 15 leaders to 'present the vision'. The Lord was undoubtedly giving vision as we did so, and the lone voice which said it was too late to pull it together was instantly contradicted by the others, who said, 'We can do it here!' or, 'We can do it there!' And so it was that three days of mission were born, starting the very next day. With less than 24 hours' notice, the first mission took place, the food arrived as promised, the team members turned up, and God moved. It was on that day that we saw four Mexican men, on different tables, in tears at the same time as God was touching their hearts. As is well known, Mexican men don't cry!

It was on Day Three, however, that the real test came, for we turned up at the park in the centre of the city and, apart from six pastors who had accompanied us throughout, there was no-one there. No team members turned up; the pastor who had promised to bring the food and organise permission had also failed to turn up. There was no mission. And yet, we all (including the Mexican pastors) had such a sense that *it must happen* that we started thinking about what might be done. I asked if we could buy some food. The locals said we could surely do a deal with a sausage vendor with a cart, already in the park. This was done in a jiffy. And so it was that the English team made an acoustic worship band, while the Mexicans distributed hot dogs to about 15 people sitting on a semicircular stone bench near where we were playing. I then felt led (with a boldness I still find extraordinary) to go up to this row of people, with Gina interpreting, to introduce ourselves and tell them about the love of God. We did this twice. And the result? Of the 25 people we spoke to, nearly all received personal prayer, 22 gave us their names and addresses and 10 of them gave their lives to Christ there and then. The other result was that a Mexican On the Move organisation was formed, backed at the highest level, to take the vision forward across the nation.

One difficulty during the year concerned finance. By early June we were about £20,000 down on where we had expected to be. The board meeting hung on, and the very next day we saw significant improvement. A mailing two weeks later to 15,000 UK team members brought a fabulous response and about £35,000 came in the post during the next month. Once again, however, by the board meeting in October, we found ourselves about £30,000 down. It was such an expensive business to keep going to country after country, and it would only take a couple of months to bring us back into crisis. Again, the board was steadfast. Later that evening, a friend and intercessor asked me what I wanted her to pray for. I said we needed money to finish the job. She asked me exactly how much money we needed. I said £30,000. She prayed there and then, and said she would continue to do so later that night. The very next day (I do not exaggerate) we received a totally unexpected (and unasked-for) promise of £30,000 – the precise amount I had asked for. Now, the *feeling* one gets when something like this happens is priceless. These moments are pure exhilaration – and I feel it now, again, as I write about it. We have a faithful God. He doesn't let his children down. He is wonderful!

An agnostic reading this might say, 'Well, it's amazing, all these things that just happen, again and again. Difficult to explain.' But I say, 'That's woolly thinking. It's not difficult to explain at all. This is a real God, who hears prayer – the God of the Bible, who promises to hear us, answering the prayer of faith and proving himself faithful. Repeated evidence like this is a challenge to each of us honestly to consider – and indeed face up to – its implications.'

As for the Christian, one could dwell on the weeks of concern about the financial position – or one can glory in the resolution of it. The point is that even the weeks of concern, which were real, were lived through in the knowledge of previous rescues. The ability to go through similar experiences subsequently is magnified by every new experience. Faith, however, still needs to be worked on. Otherwise we tend to fall back into our natural state of relying only on what we can see, as opposed to what we can remember, or what the Bible says.

There were disappointments along the way, to be sure (and I don't want to gloss over these), in terms of the capitals that didn't do the mission with us. Amsterdam had never shown much interest and, sadly, we never got to do a presentation there. Two others, which loved the vision – Istanbul and Jakarta – were so beset by persecution during 2005, especially with an anti-Christian onslaught from the Islamic media blaming the Christians publicly for all ills, that they felt they needed to lie low for a time and the missions were postponed. Gina actually had a vision of an angry Muslim woman and we felt the Lord saying that this anger was born of weakness and would pass, but that it was better not confronted. So we do feel this was probably the right thing. Brussels agreed to do the mission, but failed to get permission from the authorities for the barbecue. Meanwhile, Singapore and Tel Aviv, which had both seemed to catch the vision when we did presentations there but had yet to make a final decision, in the event said 'no'. This

caused real sadness, mainly because at this stage we could
see what the Lord was doing in each country and that it was
worthy of being received and not rejected.

The strangest moment in this respect came with
Argentina. They had conclusively invited us to come, and
yet the day before we left for South America we were told
that the Argentina mission was off. A key person there
seemed to have opposed the mission from the start. He
confirmed the invitation and then denied having done so.
Tickets bought, we had to go to Buenos Aires anyway, but
managed to get an earlier flight home. Read Luke 10.
Jesus said not everyone would receive you. It was hard,
though.

Yet 23 capital city missions did go ahead (with a
remarkable average of 14 churches and 150 team members taking part in each) and the fruit was immense,
achieved as it was through and by the ordinary believers
themselves. It is remarkable and perhaps significant that
the number of conversions recorded (3,390) matches
almost exactly the number of team members who took
part across the 23 countries (3,395). These capital city missions happened to include those of all the G8 countries, all
the largest countries by population and all the largest ones
by land area. In every sense, we had the most major capitals in the world participating. It is worth mentioning at
this point that between 2001 and 2003 I had actually tried
to get missions going in four capitals (Berlin, Madrid,
Dublin and Brussels), but not a single one of them took
place. It wasn't God's time. Yet in 2005, the time God had
planned for capital city missions, 23 took place in a single
year.

*   *   *

Excellent missions also took place in Berlin, Moscow, Ottawa, London, Delhi, Bogotá, Santiago and Cairo. Berlin was special in that it was organised for us by the German On the Move, started two years previously. Ottawa was again a lovely mission, which resulted in a Canadian On the Move organisation. A Colombian On the Move organisation was born out of the Bogotá mission. It was a similar case with Delhi. All told, by the end of the year, virtually all of the 23 nations where we had done missions were clearly continuing with vision, and 13 had at least the beginnings of a national On the Move organisation.

There were some undoubted highs. One was to see such a thing working in Moscow. How was it done there? Eighteen Baptist churches hired a river boat (obviating the need for public permission), in which about 60 believers each night invited about as many unbelievers to join them for a river cruise, over a meal (pizza!). Each cruise ended with many Russians receiving Christ and being filled with the Spirit there and then.

In one of the three mission sites in Bogotá, a truly remarkable mission happened, in that we were working that day with a single church of 60, on a Sunday morning. The church pitched up on a patch of grass across the road with chairs, tables, barbecue and worship, and went off inviting door to door and on fairly deserted streets. When the time came, enough people rolled in (about 250) to make the place buzz. 'This is lovely,' I said to Gina. There was such a wonderful sense of the presence of God and the spirited worship was a joy. (There's nothing like Latin

American worship!) The team members simply went for it, and all over you could see them praying with the guests, and many people filling in response cards. We never did any public preaching – there seemed no need. At the end, the response cards told their own story. No less than 172 people (out of about 250) had given their lives to Christ. Imagine the impact of this on a church of 60, evangelising their immediate neighbourhood during one lunchtime and seeing 172 come to Christ!

In Cairo we had our first experience of ministering in an Islamic country. Would it work? Would it even be possible to try? In the event, we experienced the most haunting of mission sites – and the most glorious of missions – in a settlement aptly nicknamed 'Garbage City'. The whole economy there is founded on the rubbish tips of Cairo, where people sift through the rubbish with their bare hands to separate plastic bottles from metal objects, etc., to process and sell on. They live in brick buildings, surrounded by this filth. The smell of the place hits one from a mile away.

There we found one of the most remarkable testimonies to the resilience of the human spirit. The people were open, warm, welcoming, totally unresentful – and they somehow just seemed to get on with life. My comment to Gina when we first saw the place was, 'I can really see now why Jesus had to be born in a stable.' There was indeed that sense of his presence in our midst as the members of the little church of 60 worshipped, as we fed our guests with simple rolls, and as we – and they – prayed for people's needs with the laying on of hands. There was such a beautiful atmosphere, almost a contradiction in terms for that place, but not quite. . . And when I asked people to indicate that they had prayed the prayer accepting Jesus, 70 Muslims – probably three quarters of those present – willingly came forward and then queued for further prayer. We will never forget that mission – and they want us back, praise God!

I want to finish the account of the 2005 missions with the stories of what happened in the two biggest countries (by population) on earth – China and India. Both were obviously strategically vital; both were the kind of places where you would ask, 'How will it possibly work here?' But work it did!

*   *   *

Entering China was in fact unproblematic and we were waved through customs without so much as a second look, three guitars and a mandolin notwithstanding (which might, after all, have been a bit of a giveaway). Our group of eight – including four 'emerging young leaders', Nick and Cristina being two of them – was met as promised by Mr N (as I shall call him), a truly delightful man in his late sixties.

When we first met this doyen of the Christian movement in China back in January, he had felt that something could be done, albeit not in its normal form. In the event, on the second day we left early for a meeting in a small town in the mountains in a fairly isolated part of Beijing District. Even here, our host veritably rushed us from the car park up the hill, through the various alleyways and into the relative sanctuary of what turned out to be a walled courtyard adjoining a simple church building. There, slightly under 60 people were waiting for us – warm-hearted peasant folk, many of whom had walked for up to five hours to get there.

Only about 15 were from the town-cum-village itself. And here were the On the Move components. First, just over 40 Christians had brought with them slightly fewer than 20 nonbelievers. (It could be done on an invitation basis, to friends who would most likely not inform on the inviters.) Second, big cauldrons of food were cooking on simple stone fireplaces in the courtyard. There was to be a meal.

Having been appraised of the likely context the night before, and knowing that many in this atheistic state might have no conception whatsoever that there might even *be* a God, I asked the Lord to show me how to speak to these people. I had a sense that I should start by reading the first chapter of Genesis. In my thinking this quickly developed into a progression from creation to the separation from God expressed in the story of the prodigal son (Luke 15). I thought later how the father's yearning for his son's return must have been even more poignant in this country with its strict one-child-only policy. Then I was going to read from John 11, the story of raising Lazarus, so that they could see the character and the love of Jesus – and then I would tell them about the crucifixion.

We had an enthusiastic audience who loved it when we brought out our instruments and sang to them. We even taught them a simple song in English, which they sang with gusto. Between each Bible reading and short talk, there was another song. Then, having preached from these Bible passages in a way I wasn't used to, and with that sense of 'flow' unceasing, I handed over to David, who re-emphasised the gospel message and led them in a prayer to receive Jesus. We were later told that 16 non-Christians had given their lives to Christ, which may have been all the non-Christians present (we can't be sure). There was certainly a wonderful atmosphere of joy in the place.

The biggest surprise came when we made ourselves available to pray for people. There was already a passion in their approach to Christ. Now, people were weeping – and in fact displaying many of the manifestations, such as shaking, associated with the 'Toronto Blessing', here in this remote mountain settlement in China. So many fell backwards ('slain in the Spirit') in response to the laying on of hands that the floor became full of people impacted powerfully by the Holy Spirit.

Then came the meal. We sat around a few tables in two sittings. When I helped myself to the delicious-looking meat stew, one of our team asked me if I'd realised what it was, staring at me from my plate. It was a chicken head – eyes, beak, brain and all! The whole stew was chicken heads. As you can imagine, our youthful team had a field day with this for the rest of the three-week trip. Meanwhile, my stomach . . . well, the less said the better.

We left with manifold hugs and such genuine fondness. It had been a remarkable day.

Mr N had clearly now decided that what we were bringing was indeed of God. Here was a man with a mobile phone and a massive network, encompassing dozens of churches, Bible colleges (which have to up sticks and change location every two weeks to keep one step ahead of the authorities) and other groupings that together make up a significant portion of the church in Beijing. Next, an upstairs restaurant premises was to be taken over in Beijing proper – hired for the evening. Again, believers were to be asked to bring friends.

The days between 'mission days' were wonderful. On the night we arrived, Mr N asked us to baptise the husband of a pastor, who had become a Christian the day before. This David did in his hotel bath! The transformation of the man's face, from before to after, was just fabulous to see. Matthew (as he was renamed that evening, according to Chinese custom) was a new man – and his wife a picture of joy.

Two days later we were doing the tourism round. David was seated next to a young man on the bus who spoke some English. He felt the Lord telling him to share his faith with this young student. Daniel, as he was renamed later that day, cancelled his plans for the day and came with us to the Imperial Gardens. This was the scene of an atrocity carried out by the British and the French in 1860, when 3,000 horsemen came and burnt down every exquisite building as a punishment to China for trying to exclude our opium sales to their increasingly addicted people. It was when Gina sensed that we should gather together and repent on behalf of our country for this gratuitously horrid act that the breakthrough came for Daniel. Thirty seconds after that prayer of repentance, Daniel said that he was ready to receive Jesus. How many spiritual strongholds in non-Christian nations relate to what the supposedly Christian ones did to them in earlier times?

Then there was the lady in the music shop whom Barbara led to Christ.

As people gathered at the restaurant on the last evening, it was a joy to see all of these people gathered there to receive us, Matthew, Daniel and the music shop woman included, along with the pastors from the mountains – all our 'old friends'. Mr N had made six phone calls and had warned us not to expect more than 30 people. Before long, he was hopping around in excitement as double that number arrived – and then more, until about 120 packed themselves in. We worshipped there with such freedom. (Freedom in the spirit was such a mark of the visit to 'unfree China'. Once, on a bus, Nick took out his mandolin and we spontaneously started singing praise songs – and the passengers clapped along in rhythm with us, wreathed in smiles. Was this really communist China?) Then, as the food was served to groups seated at round tables, I spoke, as the Lord had shown me to, from Acts 8, where Philip is sent to explain things to the eunuch, and two of the youngsters gave testimonies of God's power in their lives. When a simple gospel message was preached, at least 35 responded and a few more were led to the Lord later in the evening (encompassing nearly all the nonbelievers there). Again there was prayer ministry, though interestingly, amongst this largely student-age grouping, the direct impact on people of the Holy Spirit was much less visible than it had been in the mountains.

The key point was that it was happening – in Beijing. 'This is like revival,' said Mr N. 'I can't believe this is happening in Beijing,' said a seasoned missionary. Indeed, this missionary told me how, on arrival, she spoke to a young Chinese man who said that he had been invited there by a friend but was not himself involved in this Christianity thing. Later in the evening he bounded up to her and said, 'I'm a Christian now!' It might have been an angelic presence at the meeting that made it hard to imagine that anything *could* go wrong, in spite of an apparently strong police presence on the streets below, it being the eve of May Day, a particularly sensitive time in China. It was so easy, so natural, so joyful and so free!

Mr N and the other pastors present readily appreciated that this could be done at any time by any group of churches – simply hiring premises and inviting friends to a meal with worship and a word. This didn't prevent Mr N tackling us first thing the next (and final) day about when we would come back next year and do this in many different districts of Beijing over a week or so. A bond had been made, and all through the next couple of weeks we shared with each other how we were missing Mr N and his urgent 'come, come, come' every time we hurriedly had to board the next bus.

*   *   *

In Delhi, our team of eight gelled quickly (as usual) and we immediately found that the 26 churches, led by Pastor Daniel, had prepared superbly and in a unique manner for our visit. Not only had they put the greatest effort into making the mission as good as it could possibly be, nor had they just been imaginative about how to translate this into an Indian context, but they had also prayed with great fervour for a move of God. Which is what they got!

Imagine a big community hall, holding over 400 people seated at round tables, with a stage in the middle of one of the long sides. Imagine now the tables and chairs looking like the furniture you might expect at the plushest wedding – with white tablecloths and chairs with matching white cotton covers, with a crimson sash around each chair, tied with a bow. Then imagine professional theatre lights for the stage, a music group of about 20 producing wonderfully anointed worship music in a fully authentic Indian idiom (a breathtakingly beautiful sound). At each table, the 'host' from one of the churches had six guests who had been invited with the most beautifully produced invitation card (again wedding standard). The guests at this banquet in all numbered about 300 on each of two evenings. They were *all* Hindus, and not one (our hosts told us) had ever been to a church or, in all probability, heard anything about Jesus. Yet they had come at the invitation of their friends and the atmosphere was as attractive and loving as you can get.

What reached these unreached people was indeed love. The atmosphere (as usual carried to people's hearts through the medium of Spirit-anointed worship) was one of captivating graciousness, servanthood and compassion. Gina spoke first, sharing her heart about how Jesus was at the centre of her life. After more worship, I spoke about how Jesus healed the sick, how he healed me of cancer (what a telling testimony this had become in our evangelism!) and how he wanted to touch and bless all those present. It would be our privilege to pray for them and whatever needs they might have. I felt that a key part of my talk was to apologise (I knew I must) for the arrogant spirit in which the English had so often come to India in the past, and to explain that our desire now was to come with the heart of a servant. There was sustained applause for this.

Now, I must confess that as I went up to speak, I was saying inwardly, 'Lord, you have to help me here: I just don't know how to speak to these people.' Only the Lord could give me the words to reach people of such a different culture – all of whom, indeed, shared a different religion. A key facet of what we needed was favour, so that they would actually let us pray for them and share what we had with them. Let us, they did. Daniel first led them in a simple song, the words of which were asking Jesus to touch all our hearts. Then we offered prayer and pretty much everyone received personal prayer from their table host, from a member of the English team, or from another of the 100 or so helpers. It was a beautiful atmosphere and people were receiving the laying on of hands so willingly and gratefully.

After more worship, I spoke again and explained about our sin and how God, the creator of the universe, loved each of us as a father and sent Jesus to die on the cross to take the punishment for what each of us has done. Therefore I could be forgiven and so could they; therefore, too, the way was open for a personal relationship with the God who made us. I said that I had trusted God for everything in my life and he was there for them to trust him too; that he would lead them and fill them with his love and be their Lord for ever, even after death – having promised to raise them just as he had raised Jesus from the dead. I asked them to stand, which they each willingly did, and then (all this through an interpreter) led them in a prayer they could pray if they wanted to give their lives to Christ.

People were wreathed in smiles – and what a beautiful people they are. The dinner was served, a dinner such as most of them would apparently rarely be able to enjoy. Gina tapped me on the shoulder and said, 'Let's help with serving the food.' The local team members were astonished, and at first resistant, as we joined the others in taking plates of food to our guests. The rest of the English team were spontaneously doing the same thing.

As the evening drew to a close, I still could not have guessed what the Lord had done. Daniel spoke to each of the table leaders, who had been busy praying for their guests and then filling in contact cards for each one. 'On every table *at least* four or five [out of six] have given their lives to Christ!' That was over 200 people. The next evening, as Daniel took over the last talk and actually asked them to put their hands up if they had prayed the prayer, *virtually everyone* put their hands up, and then joined in a song of worship, many with their hands in the air. It was phenomenal. Some 550 people gave their lives to Christ in two evenings (something like 90 per cent of the non-Christians present), and by the second evening additional local pastors had come to see what was going on. All were astounded, never having experienced the like of it. The talk was of revival.

The talk was equally of the love and servanthood of Christ, which had been demonstrated and had so clearly won hearts. I have two riders to add. First, one of the most commented-on features of the evenings was that the British team members actually served at the tables. People just couldn't believe it, and couldn't stop speaking about it. After the dinner, these previously Hindu people queued up to receive more prayer and, rather than leaving once the dinner was over, mostly hung around for as much as an hour and a half afterwards. Second, Daniel told us the story of what happened two evenings later. He was in the city centre with a visitor who was buying gifts. A shopkeeper came up to Daniel and greeted him ever so warmly. 'Do you recognise me?' asked the shopkeeper. 'I'm trying to place you,' said Daniel valiantly. 'I was at the dinner,' said the shopkeeper. It turned out that this man and his colleague (quickly called over) had both given their lives to Christ. They said, 'Wait a moment,' and immediately gathered about 25 other colleagues, telling them, 'This is the father who prayed for us.' They went on to implore Daniel to pray for all the others, and to share about Jesus with them – which he duly did, in the middle of the city-centre emporium. Subsequently, Daniel told us that his church alone had 60–70 new people and he immediately had to move to two Sunday morning services.

A country more ripe for revival we have never seen. The sense that the Lord was giving them a specific tool, perfectly matched to the need, was also evident. As we parted from them, Daniel and his excellent team were already dreaming of how they would buy equipment so that hire costs could be taken out of the equation; and of how they would go about taking this 'movement' throughout Delhi and across the subcontinent of India.

18

The Bigger Picture

How can you 'live up to' a calling? How can you cope with your own weaknesses, let alone start to serve Christ?

Certainly, in my experience, it turns out to be more about who you are in Christ than about what you do, or how well you do it. The journey starts with a relationship – and pretty much ends there too.

It starts with coming to God with your sin, with your unworthiness, with your repeated capacity to mess things up, not just in the world of outcomes, but in the inner world of who you are – so that you come to know that even with the best of outcomes, you still won't measure up; and so that even the praise you receive rings hollow, because you know what you are actually like.

And into this repentance – this agony of the soul – comes the love of God, the knowledge and the percolating sweetness of sensing that you are in fact loved and infinitely valued and that you don't have to 'perform' to be so.

The healing of the heart is a gradual process. But the security of being loved (which in my case came to me as I was progressively immersed in the Holy Spirit) helps to remove the 'fear of man' – the need to succeed or impress or to adopt a persona that you think will be acceptable. Your acceptance comes from on high. And, of course, if you have a lovely spouse who is on the same journey and you have truly come to love each other, that helps greatly; and if your spouse is the type who will prick any bubble of pride and stupidity as and when presented (because he or she is also a seeker after truth and only wants the real thing), then that helps as well.

I have found God to be tremendously kind. He knows when I need to be pruned and events then serve to do this; he knows when I need to be encouraged; he knows when I need a word from him. He knows my heart and (better than I do) what I can endure. He also knows that I truly love him and want the best for his kingdom, which is real and true and perfect and eternal, and that I have little desire left for substitutes. Which is not to say that I have become any sort of an ascetic – I love a good steak, enjoy my house, like to have a debate just for the sake of it, and so on. However, there is a profound streak of 'no, that isn't real' that warns me off many a wrong track early on.

The holiness of God has sometimes seemed to people to be threatening. Its impact is actually the streamlining of what you are and what you do into the things that have worth and away from the things that are illusory. It is, you might say, common sense with spiritual eyes. Going towards other gods (whatever form they may take) is so utterly foolish when there is one who made the heavens and the earth and all good comes from him. So, keep your eyes focused. Seek first the kingdom of God and his righteousness (Matthew 6:33) – and you really can't have one without the other, for God is holy and it is from the essence of this pursuit of his *character* that you start to find his direction and his power. It is then, as you seek to be like him and to please him, that you start (in our experience, anyway) to be driven towards the life of faith; because you cannot please him, or bring glory to him (which is what you come to want to do), without doing things his way and depending on his resources. So faith proceeds from obedience, obedience from love, and love from repentance. Something like that, anyway!

As you will have seen from our story, the walk hasn't been easy, but it has been infinitely *worthwhile*. It is amazing how the wounds heal up (again, as long as you are obedient – for example, always forgive, however hard it is). The sacrifices are real, but God pays you back a thousand times (often in *this* life!). It has been a sacrifice, for example, particularly for Gina, to leave our children so much, and for them to allow us to go. But the lovely thing, as we have reached a season with much more family time, is to see that they are all in fact flourishing – which is the promise of God, but it is good to see it confirmed so readily. My dad said recently that the thing in his mind that gives the most credence to our faith (notwithstanding the cancer testimony) is the way that all four of our children have turned out. God is good!

So, it works. Of course there are dangers. The Bible is full of warnings about people who are 'puffed up' and essentially doing their own thing. Guidance is a key area here. It needs to be handled carefully, since it is so easy to say, 'God told me. . .' and then launch into a series of disasters in which God has no part. But, on the other hand, a life without guidance would for us have been a life without any of the things that have borne fruit, from the picture of the loaf of bread, to the calling to do missions in the major capitals, to the instruction to fight the court case, to the daily tweaking of direction through what we feel the Lord to be saying. It is all right not to be sure; it is all right to learn through mistakes (with an honest and fair-minded verdict on past efforts); it is OK to ask for confirmation (essential, I would say, when it's something of great moment and with great risk attached). It is especially good to operate as a twosome, which is partly why I said what I did about the importance of husbands and wives praying together.

Guidance is part of the inheritance of a Christian. We each need to learn how it is that God will guide us, and it will not necessarily be the same way he guides someone else. Simple trust, common sense and a willingness to learn are good watchwords. Gradually you do get to recognise the Father's voice.

One word on hang-ups. The Bible says repeatedly that you mustn't test God (as in Jesus' temptations, with the Israelites at the Waters of Meribah, etc.). I think what this means is that we shouldn't – mustn't – go into the venture of faith with a need to prove to ourselves that God really does love us, that he really is with us, all of which will be on the line as the step of faith is taken. That isn't faith at all – it's insecurity, tuned to manipulate God. Many people do it. I admire the response of Shadrach, Meshach and Abednego when (in Daniel 3) they are told to renounce their faith or be thrown into the fiery furnace. They say, 'If we are thrown into the blazing furnace, the God we serve is able to save us from it, and he will rescue us from your hand, O king. But even if he does not, we want you to know, O king, that we will not serve your gods. . .' (vv. 17–18). Faith springs from a healed heart, and the act of faith is not done for our own sake ('Will God back my plans, confirming his love for me?') but for his sake ('Will I follow him?'). And that, of course, has to be the nature of any calling. We start to count all things as rubbish for the sake of knowing Christ (Philippians 3:8). And he takes us at our word, often stripping much of that rubbish away. Then he starts to tell us how he wants us to serve him.

*　　*　　*

The year was done. The missions had happened. We were exhausted, but gratified – even elated – by what we had seen God do. But what had it all meant?

As a 'movement', it had already gone further than I expected. I never expected that these capital cities would resolve, one by one, to take this 'move' to the rest of their nation. I have come to grasp a particular significance of the Lord having selected capital cities for this venture. Capitals have, almost by definition, a feeling for the whole nation and a commitment to it, rather than majoring on the parochial attitude that so often reigns elsewhere. When a normal city does an On the Move mission, the chances are that they will do it again. When a capital city receives something that it believes to be of God, the natural question is, 'How can this be taken across the nation?' Virtually all the countries are clearly continuing On the Move in some form, the majority actually setting up organisations to take it nationally. So a powerful and growing movement is born, with numerous additional missions happening, in our absence, all over the world.

I truly never anticipated that this single vision could be so suitable to every country to which it was taken. How can the same simple thing work in China, Kenya and Australia? To put it another way, how can the same thing be right in communities that are historically Protestant, Roman Catholic, Orthodox, Buddhist/Shintoist, Hindu, Muslim, atheistic, communist, or just money mad? How can God design a single concept to be revolutionary and uniquely effective in *every* culture to which it has been introduced? This is a miracle. It is also a significant pointer to something: it isn't barbecues that have done this, it is a move of the Holy Spirit, who is able to transcend cultural differences and speak to hearts and situations, irrespective of location and culture.

So what can we learn about this move of the Spirit, about what God is doing, about what is in his heart? It is here that we get to the heart of the matter.

First, I want to say something about England. I do believe that God has a special destiny for my country; that the trail that was blazed in the last three centuries by the English (and indeed the Scots, Welsh and Irish) all over the world has, by God's decree, set paths that can be retraced and relationships that can be reawakened for his glory. We British have a unique heritage and a unique opportunity, to which we must now rise. We are to take a lead and the nations of the world are actually looking to us to do so. This will have to be enacted in weakness, because our erstwhile strength is simply not there any more. But God's strength is made perfect in our weakness, and the servant heart must replace the exercise of power as the medium in which we operate. Once rulers, we are now called to be the servants of all.

Second, as nations start to unite under the banner of the gospel, God is bringing the world church into a new place of authority. If the 'prayer of agreement' is key to our exercising authority in prayer, then the fault-lines that have divided race, nation and denomination from each other have sapped our authority as a church, and have made us victims of world forces rather than the shapers thereof. Only the church can break out of the world's divisive mentality. Only in the church can one travel to nation after nation and find an instant family bond, a bond that within each nation is equally coming to transcend both denomination and race and which is part of the glory of the God we serve. Everything is in place for the world church to become one, truly. God is calling us into that destiny now. We must rise to it. Together, we are the body of Christ. Together, we are a force to be reckoned with. Together, we have the spiritual authority we crave.

Third, I believe that the unity we seek has to be based on equality between the nations. I think that God is calling into being a family of nations in which no-one is the leader. The other day, someone had a picture of an athletics stadium with the athletes running around the main track. Rather than there being a winner, all the runners were running in a line – in formation, as it were; each one was followed by an angel, who carried the flag of that particular runner's nation; they were running in concert; and the crowd in the stadium was applauding and cheering *all of them* as they ran together to finish the race. This does not mean that Britain is not to have a role in bringing something of this to pass – but it is a servant role, where leadership is destined to be given away.

This leads me to something about the character of Christ. What is the 'glory' of the Lord? His greatest glory is his servanthood. What I mean is this. Jesus said, 'If anyone wants to be first, he must be the very last, and the servant of all' (Mark 9:35). Again, 'Therefore, whoever humbles himself like this child is the greatest in the kingdom of heaven' (Matthew 18:4). This is what Jesus did, as well as said: 'Whoever wants to become great among you must be your servant, and whoever wants to be first must be your slave – just as the Son of Man did not come to be served, but to serve, and to give his life as a ransom for many' (Matthew 20:26–28). God's glory is that he did this: he, who was all powerful and had no need of anyone, willingly sacrificed himself out of love for the broken, the useless, the selfish and the sinful. Why should he have done this? It is his glory that he did so:

> Who, being in very nature God,
> > did not consider equality with God something to be
> > grasped,
> but made himself nothing,
> > taking the very nature of a servant,
> > being made in human likeness.
> And being found in appearance as a man,
> > he humbled himself
> > and became obedient to death – even death on a cross!

Therefore God exalted him to the highest place
   and gave him the name that is above every name,
that at the name of Jesus every knee should bow,
   in heaven and on earth and under the earth,
and every tongue confess that Jesus Christ is Lord,
   to the glory of God the Father.
   (Philippians 2:6–11, my italics)

And so, when in Revelation it is asked who is worthy to break the seals and open the scroll, and John weeps because no-one is found who is worthy, he is told, 'Do not weep! See, the Lion of the tribe of Judah, the Root of David, has triumphed. He is able to open the scroll and its seven seals' (5:5). Then he sees a Lamb, looking as if it had been slain (v. 6), and they sing a new song:

You are worthy to take the scroll
   and to open its seals,
because you were slain,
   and with your blood you purchased men for God
   from every tribe and language and people and nation.
You have made them to be a kingdom and priests to serve
   our God,
   and they will reign on the earth. (vv. 9–10)

Jesus served – and that was his glory. And he wants us to serve too.

Now, this runs against the prevailing culture. The darkness – 'See, darkness covers the earth and thick darkness is over the peoples' (Isaiah 60:2) – is increasingly pervasive, and I believe that no amount of talk about 'Christian values' will shift it. We are no longer understood. In this

darkness the people have come to speak another language.

What is the way through this darkness? Isaiah goes on to
say, 'But the LORD rises upon you and his glory appears over
you' (v. 2b). And what is his glory? That he came to serve
and not to be served.

Here, I believe, is the clue for the church. I think we are
powerless to shift the darkness by arguing against its precepts. But the glory of the Lord rises upon us as we do what
he did, and what he now calls us to do. This is to give ourselves for others; truly to love; truly to serve the world in
which we find ourselves. The church is so *attractive* when
it begins to serve. We have seen this again and again,
whether in India or Canada. Oh, that we in the church
would 'get it' and start to give ourselves for others! Isaiah
58:9–10 says,

> If you do away with the yoke of oppression,
>   with the pointing finger and malicious talk,
> and if you spend yourselves on behalf of the hungry,
>   and satisfy the needs of the oppressed,
> then your light will rise in the darkness,
>   and your night will become like the noonday.

I believe this must be done in the power of the Spirit, not
'in the flesh'.

> The Spirit of the Sovereign LORD is on me,
>   because the LORD has anointed me
>   to preach good news to the poor.
> He has sent me to bind up the broken-hearted,
>   to proclaim freedom for the captives

and release from darkness for the prisoners.
(Isaiah 61:1–2)

It is in the power of the Spirit that we can 'break every yoke' (58:6). And it is in the power of the Spirit that we can truly love, because 'God has poured out his love into our hearts by the Holy Spirit' (Romans 5:5).

Even the 'coolest', the most 'gangster' individuals respond to love. It meets their deepest need, melts their hearts and is unstoppable. We have found that the church is held in great favour as we go out and minister to people, give of our best to them, and seek to serve. All over the world, this captures hearts like nothing else. And, more than being an evangelistic tool which 'gets results', a servant-hearted ministry stands on its head the very things that we have come to think the church is 'for'. It is not about results; it is not about becoming larger and stronger through successful campaigns. It is about following the example of our Saviour, who gave everything for others. We only have to give, to love and to serve, unconditionally. Then his glory rises upon us, because by our actions and our alignment of heart we are partaking in that glory. The point is not to seek to build our institutions, but to *sacrifice* them, and ourselves, for the sake of the ones he created and still loves. We must become weak; we must become nothing; we must humble ourselves; we must serve others. In that way, our lights will rise in the darkness and our night – and their night – will become like the noonday. I have seen it in action.

To counter the prevailing spirit, we must therefore speak – and act out – the language of love, in the power of the

Holy Spirit. This demonstration of love must be international in its scope, for international enmity and pride have scarred the church, along with the rest of society, and have denied it the oneness that is the fruit and the prerequisite of love. Nation must serve nation. Equally, denomination must serve denomination, and race must serve race. This is part of the 'big picture' where the victory is won, which then allows beautiful expressions of that victory (downstream, as it were) in every individual life.

Isaiah speaks of raising 'a banner' to which 'the nations will rally' (11:10). A banner is, by definition, highly visible. This banner is Jesus; but it is also the church, in unity, moving in the love of Jesus and exhibiting his character in what it does – overtly, for all to see. 'Let your light shine before men, that they may see your good deeds and praise your Father in heaven' (Matthew 5:16). The banner is love; it is unity; it is doing the things that Jesus did and now wants to do through us; it is doing it publicly, a 'city on a hill' (5:14); and it is international, for how else could the nations rally to it?

There is surely a compelling agenda here. Jesus only did the things he saw his Father doing. What is the Father doing? He is reaching out; he is mobilising his church; a massive army is in the process of being awakened; he is teaching us how to give, how to abandon the world's agenda of success and respond to his agenda of self-sacrifice and love. He is making us more like Jesus, 'to be conformed to the image of his Son, in order that he might be the first-born among many brethren' (Romans 8:29 RSV). This army will be unstoppable. But it must be mobilised, and quickly, for the darkness is closing in and the comfortable complacency of much of the church is ultimately – soon – a place of peril, not safety. As the darkness gets darker, there can be no middle ground. This is the challenge to a sleeping church:

> Arise, shine, for your light has come,
>   and the glory of the Lord rises upon you. (Isaiah 60:1)

The challenge is for the church, which is called by his name, to act like him; the challenge is to waken to his call and, together, to prepare the way for his imminent return.

Postscript

In September 2004, while I was in India preparing to present the vision, I believe the Lord highlighted something for me at the end of the story of Gideon:

The Israelites said to Gideon, 'Rule over us – you, your son and your grandson – because you have saved us out of the hand of Midian.'

But Gideon told them, 'I will not rule over you, nor will my son rule over you. The LORD will rule over you.' And he said, 'I do have one request, that each of you give me an ear-ring from your share of the plunder.' (It was the custom of the Ishmaelites to wear gold ear-rings.)

They answered, 'We'll be glad to give them.' So they spread out a garment, and each man threw a ring from his plunder onto it. The weight of the gold rings he asked for came to seventeen hundred shekels . . . Gideon made the gold into an ephod, which he placed in Ophrah, his town. All Israel prostituted themselves by worshipping it there, and it became a snare to Gideon and his family. (Judges 8:22–27)

I think that God gave me these verses as a warning, even before the missions of 2005 had taken place. Gideon did amazing things, under God, and innocent-seeming thanks became a most serious snare – to the people and to Gideon and his family. There is a danger with a story like this about the exploits of God through individuals, that people will look at an achievement and, as it were, worship it – rather than worshipping the God who wrought it. Concentrating on the acts of our story, without those acts pointing us to the God who enabled them – and who can enable any acts, at any time – would similarly be a snare, to all of us. To God *must* go *all* the glory.

For Further Information

On the Move would be pleased to hear from you. Our contact details are:

On the Move
PO Box 7761
Birmingham
B17 OBW
UK
Tel: (0044) 121 427 3300

Email: onthemove@btinternet.com
Website: www.onthemove.org.uk

On the website, you will find brief reports, with pictures, for all of the capital city missions of 2005. You will also find a schedule of current and forthcoming missions in the UK and internationally. You'd be most welcome to 'come and see'.

We have a DVD which has 37 minutes of video footage from the 2005 capital city missions, which really makes missions you have read about 'come alive'. This is available from OTM, price £8 including p&p.

We exist to serve the church. If you feel we might be able to help the churches in your area through an On the Move mission, please feel free to make contact. That's what we're here for.